"Marie Noonan Sabin has written a book that fills a gap in Teilhard Studies, that is, the place of Scripture in his evolutionary paradigm. By bringing together Teilhard's emergence of the ultrahuman and wisdom literature she draws out, in a beautiful and deep way, the consonance between Teilhard's Christic vision and the scriptural vision of human becoming. Contrary to some of his critics, Sabin affirms that Teilhard's insights were deeply biblical and Christian. I highly recommend this book for those interested in a biblical exegesis of Teilhard's incarnational vision."

—Ilia Delio, OSF
Josephine C. Connelly Endowed Chair in Theology
Villanova University

"Marie Sabin insightfully employs aspects of Teilhard's concept of developing human consciousness to interpret biblical texts. She does not claim that 'Teilhardian' themes lie nascent with the texts themselves, but that Teilhard's interpretive lenses open up a 'surplus of meaning.' For example, the notion of an evolving creation throws light on the mystery of human suffering in Job; the idea of unifying consciousness enhances the New Testament understanding of human divinization. His way of reading opens the Bible in intriguing ways."

—Dianne Bergant, CSA
Professor Emerita of Old Testament Studies
Catholic Theological Union

Evolving Humanity and Biblical Wisdom

Reading Scripture through the Lens of Teilhard de Chardin

Marie Noonan Sabin

LITURGICAL PRESS
ACADEMIC

Collegeville, Minnesota
www.litpress.org

Cover design by Ann Blattner. "Pentecost," painting by Fr. Arthur Poulin, Incarnation Monastery, Berkeley, California.

1   2   3   4   5   6   7   8   9

Library of Congress Cataloging-in-Publication Data

Names: Sabin, Marie Noonan, author.
Title: Evolving humanity and biblical wisdom : reading scripture through the lens of Teilhard de Chardin / Marie Noonan Sabin.
Description: Collegeville, Minnesota : Liturgical Press, 2018.
Identifiers: LCCN 2017037230 (print) | LCCN 2017055560 (ebook) | ISBN 9780814684528 | ISBN 9780814684771 (ebook)
Subjects: LCSH: Bible—Criticism, interpretation, etc. | Teilhard de Chardin, Pierre. | Theology.
Classification: LCC BS511.3 .S225 2018 (print) | LCC BS511.3 (ebook) | DDC 220.6092—dc23
LC record available at https://lccn.loc.gov/2017037230

Contents

Introduction

Is Humanity Still Evolving?

In April 2017 the cover of the *National Geographic* showed a series of faces from ape to human to something not yet seen; it was titled "The Next Human." Inside, in an article titled "Beyond Human," D. T. Max states matter-of-factly:

> Until recently it was thought that our species had stopped evolving far in the past. Our ability to peer inside the human genome has shown that in fact our biology continues to change to suit particular environments. (45)

In particular, he quotes the work of Ray Kurzwell in *The Singularity Is Near* (New York: Viking Press, 2005): "We will transcend all of the limitations of our biology. That is what it means to be human—to extend who we are" (48). In the bulk of the article Max focuses on what human beings can do (and have already done) to use technology to extend human capabilities. He discusses machines that compensate for human defects and genetic engineering that can alter animals and insects so that they can no longer host the bacteria that cause human disease. He speculates about the future possibilities of customizing an embryo. In doing so, he notes the ethical dilemma it raises, citing the questions of bioethicist Linda MacDonald Glenn: "What becomes the new norm as we try to improve ourselves? . . . You might enhance people to make them smarter, but does smarter equal better or happier?" (59).

Teilhard de Chardin would have found this discussion unsurprising. Sixty years ago he was arguing that "when observed through a sufficient depth of time (millions of years) Life can be seen to move. Not only does it move but it advances in a definite direction. In any period of ten million years Life practically grows a new skin."[1]

This "new skin" Teilhard names as "the *cerebralization* of living creatures." He points out:

> Research shows that from the lowest to the highest level of the organic world there is a persistent and clearly defined thrust of animal forms towards species with more sensitive and elaborate nervous systems. . . . There is an amphibian phase of the brain, a reptile phase, a mammal phase. . . . What else can this mean except that, as shown by the nervous systems, there is an emotional heightening, a rising tide of consciousness.[2]

Teilhard then asks where humanity—as a species—is to be located in respect to this general evolution in consciousness. His response:

> If, as I maintain, the movement of the cosmos towards the highest degree of consciousness is not an optical illusion, but represents the essence of biological evolution, then, in the curve traced by [biological] Life, Humankind is unquestionably situated at the topmost point. . . . Does not the birth of Thought stand out as a critical point through which all striving of previous ages passes and is consummated—the critical point . . . when, by force of concentration, it ends by reflecting upon itself?[3]

1. *The Future of Man*, trans. Norman Denney (New York: Harper and Row, 1964), 64–65.
2. *Future of Man*, 65.
3. *Future of Man*, 67.

Teilhard sums up the implications of his observations as follows:

> Progress = growth of consciousness
> Growth of consciousness = effect of organization[4]

Distinguishing between an individual human being and collective humanity, Teilhard finds no perceptible progress in the first but unmistakable advances in the second, all of them manifest in terms of greater and greater organization:

> Economic concentration, manifest in the unification of the earth's energies.
> Intellectual concentration, manifest in the unification of knowledge in a coherent system (science).
> Social concentration, manifest in a unification of the human mass as a thinking whole.[5]

One can only imagine how Teilhard would feel proven right by how we are moving today: towards a global economy, global concern for the climate, global exchanges of knowledge, and a global system of communication. Yet he also felt in 1941 that humanity was at a critical crossroads. Confronted by the horrors of World War II, he asked, "Have we not reached a dead-end? Can we talk seriously of a future for Humankind?"[6] If he asked that question then, how much more might he ask it now?

Even so, I am sure that now, as then, he would answer in a positive way. He would do so, first, on the basis of recent advances in human thought, in particular the growing human acknowledgment of the interconnectedness of all things: Human well-being with the well-being of plants and animals and the Earth as a

---

4. *Future of Man*, 69.
5. *Future of Man*.
6. *Future of Man*, 70.

whole, and, most of all, the well-being of one group of human beings with all the others on the planet. Teilhard died before the development of the internet. He would surely have seen it as a confirmation of his vision of the development of the collective human brain and the global convergence of human thought.

His enthusiasm for every aspect of human development made him a humanist in the full sense of the word. And that robust humanism affected his deep religious faith, causing him to perceive an essential unity between science and religion in a period when others saw only a divide. He summed up the key question of that divide as follows: "Are we to disdain the world and put it behind us, or live in it in order to master and perfect it?"[7] For his own part, he envisioned and urged their merger:

> Faith in God and faith in the World: these two springs of energy, each the source of a magnificent spiritual impulse, must certainly be capable of effectively uniting in such a way as to produce a resulting upward movement.[8]

Teilhard saw that if the religious believer accepted this idea of evolution, "there would follow a radical incorporation of terrestrial values in the most fundamental concepts of his Faith." The most significant of these concepts would be that of charity:

> The love of God expresses and crowns the basic affinity which, from the beginning of Time and Space, has drawn together and concentrated the "spiritualizable" elements of the Universe. To love God and our neighbor is not merely an act of worship and compassion superimposed on other individual preoccupations. For the Christian, if he be truly Christian, it is Life itself.[9]

7. *Future of Man*, 77.
8. *Future of Man*.
9. *Future of Man*, 79.

It is the conjunction of Science's idea of biological growth in spiritual energy with Religion's idea of spiritual growth in spiritual energy that formed Teilhard's vision:

> The sense of the earth opening and exploding upwards into God, and the sense of God taking root and finding nourishment downwards into Earth. A personal, transcendent God and an evolving Universe no longer forming two hostile centers of attraction, but entering into hierarchic conjunction to raise the human mass on a single tide.[10]

Teilhard speaks specifically out of his own Christian faith. For him, Christ represented the supreme breakthrough and model of human evolution. But he did not exclude others from arriving at this "higher level of consciousness":

> Whether Christian or non-Christian, the people inspired by this particular conviction [that is, of the spiritual evolution of humanity toward oneness], constitute a homogenous category. Though they may be situated at two extreme wings of Humankind on earth [that is, Science and Religion], they can advance unequivocally side by side because their attitudes, far from being mutually exclusive, are virtually an extension one of the other and ask only to be completed.[11]

The Biblical Roots of Teilhard's Vision

Although Teilhard does not take the Bible as his starting point, his perspective nonetheless contains a mystical vision rooted in the Jewish and Christian Scriptures. I would like to take note of

---

10. *Future of Man*, 80.

11. *Future of Man*. Thomas Merton praised Teilhard for the "effort to reconvert the scientific view of the cosmos into a wisdom." See Christopher Pramuk, *Sophia: The Hidden Christ of Thomas Merton* (Collegeville, MN: Liturgical Press, 2009), 147n75.

some of the scriptural passages behind it—especially his mystical work, *The Divine Milieu.*

Among those of first importance is Jacob's dream. After Jacob had received his father's blessing and journeys to find a wife, he rests for the night. Then "he dreamed that there was a ladder set up on earth, the top of it reaching to heaven; and the angels of God were ascending and descending on it." What happens next is what catches Teilhard's attention:

> Then Jacob awoke from his sleep and said, "Surely the Lord is in this place—and I did not know it!" And he was afraid, and said, "How awesome is this place! This is none other than the house of God, and this is the gate of heaven!" (Gen 28:16-17)

Teilhard interprets this passage to mean that the material world in which we live is sacred. Matter is holy. The world of matter is "the house of God" and "the gate of heaven." It is "the divine milieu":

> As Jacob said, awakening from his dream, the world, this palpable world, which we were wont to treat with the boredom and disrespect with which we habitually regard places with no sacred association for us, is in truth a holy place, and we did not know it.[12]

For Teilhard, Jacob's insight is basic to being fully human; we need to perceive that "God reveals himself everywhere."[13] For Teilhard, this way of seeing is not reserved for special moments of grace, or restricted to special places, persons, actions, or prayers. It is simply the way human beings are meant to understand everything in their lives. Teilhard speaks of this as "divinization"—that is, a way of perceiving, and making, all things human to be holy.

---

12. *The Divine Milieu*, trans. William Collins (New York: Harper Perennial, 2001), 83–84.

13. *Divine Milieu*, 85.

He believed that "transfiguration" is how every human person is meant to grow towards God. He sees the transformation or transfiguration of matter into spirit, or the human into the divine, or the natural into the supernatural, as the end point or omega of human evolution. Human endeavors, human interests, human loves, and even human losses are to be embraced wholeheartedly because they are the way to God. Ultimately, God will transform—transfigure—every aspect of our humanity into divine Being. Teilhard sees the common contrast between spirit and matter or soul and body as a "crude illusion." He speaks instead of "holy matter" and advises that that it not be regarded as a "burden" to be shunned but instead prized as a means of growth. Created things, he says, are not obstacles to the divine but "footholds" by which we ascend to God.[14]

Central to Teilhard's understanding of this process of human transformation is the reality of divine being manifest in the human Christ. "Let us examine step by step," he says, "how we can validate to ourselves this prodigious identification of the Son of Man and the divine milieu."[15] It is worth noting that he uses "Son of Man" not as a title signifying divinity but as a term emphasizing Christ's humanity.[16] It is the coexistence of divinity and humanity that seizes him: it is a "prodigious identification." Accepting its reality in Christ means, for Teilhard, accepting its possibility for everyone:

> Under what form, and with what end in view, has the Creator given us, and still preserves in us, the gift of participated being? Under the form of an essential aspiration towards him—and with a view to the unhoped-for cleaving which is to make us one and the same complex thing with

14. *Divine Milieu*, 75–77.

15. *Divine Milieu*, 94.

16. Because I believe that when the evangelists use the term, they, too, had its Hebrew meaning in mind—that is, "son of Adam" or "human being"—I have purposefully *not* capitalized the phrase throughout this book.

him. The action by which God maintains us in the field of his presence is *a unitive transformation.*[17]

In support of this perspective, Teilhard calls on Paul and John:

> What is the supreme and complex reality for which the divine operation molds us? It is revealed to us by St. Paul and St. John. It is the quantitative repletion and the qualitative consummation of all things: it is the mysterious Pleroma [the Fullness], in which the substantial one, and the created many, fuse without confusion in a whole which, without adding anything essential to God, will nevertheless be a sort of triumph and generalization of being.[18]

The reference to the "Pleroma" suggests that Teilhard was thinking of the Pauline Letter to the Colossians and the Prologue of John's gospel. From Colossians, he must have had in mind the passage that speaks of Christ as "the image of the invisible God" and continues, "For in him all the fullness of God was pleased to dwell" (Col 1:15, 19). From John, the allusion is to the end of the Prologue: "From his fullness we have all received, grace from grace" (John 1:16). The idea of Christ as the *fullness* of Creation blended in Teilhard's mind with his scientific understanding of how the universe is expanding, and humanity is evolving, towards fullness of Being.

Teilhard saw the fullness of Christ as the omega point of evolution, and each person as a cocreator in this evolutionary process. He believed that each person

> must build—starting with the natural territory of his own self—a work, an opus, into which something enters from all the elements of the earth. He makes his own soul throughout all his earthly days; and at the same time he collaborates in another work, another opus which infinitely transcends, while at the same time it narrowly determines, the perspec-

17. *Divine Milieu*, 94–95.
18. *Divine Milieu*, 95.

tives of his individual achievement: the completing of the world. . . . Through our efforts to put spiritual form into our own lives, the world slowly accumulates, starting with the whole of matter, that which will make of it the Heavenly Jerusalem or the New Earth.[19]

Teilhard sees human beings completing not only the first creation but also what he deems the second creation, the incarnation of Christ—which, for him, represents the full integration of matter with spirit, humanity with divinity. He says, "With each one of our *works*, we labor—in individual separation, but no less really—to build the Pleroma, that is to say, we bring to Christ a little fulfillment."[20]

"Bringing Christ to fulfillment" means, for Teilhard, a two-way process: it involves both the divinization of the human and humanization of the divine. It is his firm insistence on the union of these two dimensions that distinguishes Teilhard's spirituality from more conventional forms. He does not advocate either renouncing the world or staying apart from it. He sees involvement in the world, in matter, in human things, as part of the work of God. Teilhard sees all things human as part of the evolutionary process that leads to God through God's power of transformation.

For Teilhard what matters is the capacity to see the divine in the human, just as the disciples did in the moment of Christ's transfiguration. He believes that the perception of God's presence in every person is what will make universal charity possible in the world, and that state of universal charity is the omega of evolution:

> The only subject ultimately capable of mystical transfiguration is the whole group of mankind forming a single body and a single soul in charity.[21]

19. *Divine Milieu*, 24.
20. *Divine Milieu*, 26.
21. *Divine Milieu*, 121.

It is this universal love of others, based on the perception of the divine presence in them, that defines for Teilhard the meaning of Christ's "Second Coming."

Teilhard thinks that the attitude of "expectation"—that is, of hope—is "perhaps the supreme Christian function and the most distinctive characteristic of our religion."[22] And he thinks this hope must be for humanity as a whole, not just one segment of it:

> The Israelites were constantly expectant, and the first Christians, too. . . . The Messiah, who appeared for a moment in our midst, only allowed himself to be seen and touched for a moment before vanishing once again, more luminous and ineffable than ever, into the depths of the future. He came. Yet now we must expect him—no longer a small chosen group among us, but all men—once again, and more than ever.[23]

These are some of the key passages that reveal the scriptural roots of Teilhard's perspective. From the Old Testament, Teilhard refers directly to Jacob and Job and seems to have Isaiah in the back of his mind. From the New Testament, he quotes frequently from Paul and sometimes from John, and he alludes broadly to the other gospels. Central to his thought is the transfiguration of Christ, which he sees as predictive for all humanity. He understands both the cross and Christ's "second coming" in the light of the transfiguration. His ultimate emphasis is on the need for a different way of seeing: a way of seeing human achievement, human suffering, and human expectation; a way of mystical insight that he finds in Scripture and melds with the science of evolution. Teilhard closes the gap between science and religion because, in his view, each points to one and the same ending.

22. *Divine Milieu*, 130.
23. *Divine Milieu*.

The Aim of This Book

As one focused on a way of seeing, Teilhard is essentially concerned with human wisdom. In the chapters that follow, I select biblical passages connected with wisdom and undertake to read them through Teilhard's evolutionary lens. I have found new meaning in them by going back to them in the light of his view of spiritual evolution. That is hardly surprising. Every generation brings its current cosmology to its religious understanding and, as cosmology has changed so has scriptural interpretation. Shifts in science have helped keep the biblical word a living word.

I begin with Job, considering not only his question—"Where shall Wisdom be found?"—but also the existential angst that prompted it: If God is just and Job is innocent, why should Job suffer? I argue that the wisdom the work has to offer is linked both to the nature of an evolving creation and to an evolving idea of God. In another chapter I try to show how some early texts, dated just before and after the first century, fostered the idea of human beings breaking through the conventional limits of humanity to share in the life of divinity. They do not, of course, speak of this as "evolution," but the idea is implicit. The following chapter deals with the sanctification of God's Word and the personification of divine Wisdom in Judaism. Here again I find an evolutionary process at work: first, because God's Word is assigned mystical properties in Judaism; second, because Wisdom is imagined as a woman who cocreates with God; and third, because the characteristics of both this mystical Word and personified Wisdom are later embodied in the Christ envisioned in both the gospels and the Creed.

As a further exploration of how much the Christian tradition is imbued with Jewish, mystical notions of divine and embodied Wisdom, I consider how Christ is described as Wisdom and how Wisdom language provides a mystical dimension to each gospel: riddling proverb and parable in Mark, God's word "re-actualized" in Matthew, God's Wisdom as God's "Holy Spirit" in Luke, and

God's Wisdom (or Word) made flesh in the mystical speech of John. Last of all, I explore the extent to which the gospels summon their readers to evolve into a Word of God themselves—that is, to the mystical transformation of becoming, as it were, *flesh made Word*. In that connection, I look at the various ways the gospels are unfinished and create the expectation of something more to come.

In conclusion, I reflect on how these Scriptures reveal and support the idea of evolving humanity, but with an important twist. Reading the Scriptures through Teilhard's lens poses a new way of seeing the relationship between "the spirit" and "the world." In past ages, biblical expressions of sharing in divinity have been understood to mean withdrawal from the world; in Teilhard's perspective, they point, instead, towards wholehearted engagement. In particular, he fosters the kind of engagement that comes with empathy. Teilhard envisioned all humanity coming together in a unifying consciousness that he called "Christ-consciousness." He had a vision of a "re-born Christianity . . . capable of becoming the Religion of Evolution."[24] In that vision he saw all people coming together in a global, empathetic understanding and love.

24. *The Heart of Matter*, trans. René Hague (New York: Harcourt Brace Jovanovich, 1978), 99.

1

Job and the Evolution of God

> "All around us, and within our own selves,
> God is in the process of 'changing,' as the result
> of the coincidence of his magnetic power and our
> own thought."[1]

Among the many horrifying images of Elie Wiesel's *Night* is the hanging of a young child in the Nazi camp. Forced to watch, one of the inmates cries out, "Where is merciful God? Where is He?" As the child lingers between life and death, the same man asks again, "For God's sake, where is God?" And Wiesel hears a voice within him, saying, "Where He is? This is where— hanging here from this gallows."[2] The answer is both enigmatic and profound. The book of Job raises the same question and insinuates the same response.

The name *Job* has been variously interpreted to mean "enemy" or "Where [is] the father?" The sharp disparity between these two meanings is the result of different

---

1. Teilhard de Chardin, *The Heart of Matter*, trans. René Hague (New York: Harcourt Brace Jovanovich, 1978), 53.
2. *Night* (New York: Hill and Wang, 2006), 64–65.

choices of Hebrew vowels that are not present in the ancient text and so have to be inserted by the reader. Readers who see Job's plight as evidence that God has attacked him as though he were an enemy, or who note that Job at times comes to think of God as an enemy, choose the first meaning. Those who choose the second perceive Job's central question to be an existential exploration of what it means to regard God as a father—the *Yahweh* that ancient Jewish prayers proclaim.

It is possible to see some justification for both. In fact, it might be argued that the deep texture of the work lies in its ambiguity, its allowance for shifting points of view. Multiple ways in which human beings have tended to conceptualize God are dramatized by the author, from the simplistic, folktale God of the opening, through the conventional and limited arguments of Job's comforters, to the complex and mysterious God of the ending. Through it all, Job's anguish and the questions that arise from it probe the viability of each stance. Is God an enemy to Job, or a caring father? Or does Job's perception of God evolve from one to the other?

Once dated early in the Hebrew canon, the book of Job is now assigned to postexilic times—sixth to fifth century BCE—when, as in post-Holocaust times, the question of God's presence became paramount. This dating is confirmed by the numerous parallels and allusions to the Psalms, in particular postexilic psalms of lament.

The very structure of the book of Job loosely follows the structure of a lament psalm, as outlined by Walter Brueggemann.[3] In Brueggemann's analysis, the lament psalm often starts in one emotional place and ends in another: it moves from a state of dislocation to reorientation. So, for example, Psalm 22 begins with an expression of despair—"My God, my God, why have you abandoned me?"—yet ends on a note of praise and proclamation of God's saving power. Somewhere in the middle, there is a cry for help on the part of the psalmist and then a hiatus, a space that

---

3. *Praying the Psalms* (Eugene, OR: Cascade Books, 2007), 8–11, 23–24.

allows for the action of grace. In the case of Psalm 22, the cry for help occurs in verses 19-21a:

> But you, O LORD, do not be far away!
>   O my help, come quickly to my aid!
> Deliver my soul from the sword,
>   my life from the power of the dog!
> Save me from the mouth of the lion!

This cry for help also contains an implicit expression of faith that God *can* and *will* help. A hiatus follows; there is no narrative to bridge the gap between that cry and the next words of the psalmist. Abruptly we hear the psalmist saying, "From the horns of the wild oxen you have rescued me" (21b). Grace has intervened. God appears present once more and the psalmist praises him (22-31).

In the same way, the book of Job begins with Job's lament—one that, in this case, carries on for many chapters, with varying expressions of despair. Nonetheless, at the end of chapter 19, Job gives voice to a remarkable expression of faith:

> For I know that my Vindicator lives,
>   and that at the last he will stand upon the earth;
> and after my skin has been thus destroyed,
>   then in my flesh I shall see God,
> whom I shall see on my side,
>   and my eyes shall behold, and not another. (19:25-27)[4]

The Hebrew text of these verses is difficult and uncertain in places, but what comes through clearly is the speaker's faith in a God who is ultimately just and whom Job will ultimately see. His faith in being able to see God is repeated three times, and this form

---

4. This follows the NRSV translation with the exception of "Vindicator." The NRSV gives "Redeemer" as first choice and then (inexplicably) notes that "Vindicator" would be better. "Vindicator" is also the choice of *The Jewish Study Bible*, edited by Adele Berlin and Marc Zvi Brettler, with Michael Fishbane (New York: Oxford University Press, 2004).

of faith is significant in a work that wrestles with the question of how God relates to human beings. This passage performs the same function as verses 19-21a in Psalm 22. What follows in the book of Job, however, is not an immediate hiatus but many more chapters of Job's complaint and false solutions given by his so-called comforters. Finally, some nineteen chapters later, God does respond to Job's act of faith and appears to him (chap. 38). At the very end of the work, Job acknowledges this direct experience: "I had heard of you by the hearing of the ear, but now my eye sees you" (42:5).

This brief overview of the structure of the book of Job does not take into account the speeches of Elihu in chapters 32–37 (which many consider a later addition), the inconsistencies in Job's varying expressions of trust and despair, or the significance of the prose frame for his story. But it is enough, I hope, to suggest that this long, complex, and unwieldy book does bear some structural relationship to the psalms of lament and contains, as they do, a drama of faith that starts in one place and ends in another.

The book of Job is also indebted to the Psalms for much of its content. The psalms of lament comprise one-third of the psalter, and the situation of undeserved misery and near despair in which Job finds himself has many parallels. Psalm 17, for example, contains the same plea for justice and vindication—"Hear a just cause, O LORD, . . . From you let my vindication come" (vv. 1-2)—and the same demand that God respond to the speaker:

> I call upon you, for you will answer me, O God (v. 6)

> I shall behold your face in righteousness;
> I shall be satisfied, beholding your likeness. (v. 15)

Psalm 26, like both Psalm 17 and Job, insists on the innocence of the sufferer: "Vindicate me, O LORD, for I have walked in my integrity" (v. 1).

Psalm 31 indicates that the speaker suffers the same kind of social alienation as Job:

My life is spent with sorrow . . .
I am the scorn of all my adversaries,
    a horror to my neighbors,
an object of dread to my acquaintances. (vv. 10-11)

Psalm 42 (vv. 3, 10) twice repeats the phrase "Where is your God?" In context, this question is part of the ridicule of the psalmist's enemies. The echo here suggests that in Job's case, as in that of the psalmist, God's reputation is at stake in Job's final outcome.

Occasionally, the psalmist—again like Job in certain places—accuses God of being the enemy. In Psalm 22 the speaker says to God, "You lay me in the dust of death" (v. 15), and in Psalm 102:

All day long my enemies taunt me . . .
For I eat ashes like bread,
    and mingle tears with my drink,
because of your indignation and anger;
    for you have lifted me up and thrown me aside. (vv. 8-10)

In many other psalms, God may not be exactly the enemy but is surely hiding his face. In Psalm 69:17, for example, the psalmist implores God, "Do not hide your face from your servant," and in Psalm 143:7, he says, "Do not hide your face from me, or I shall be like those who go down to the Pit." Job's insistence that he see God's face thus takes its place among a long legacy of similar pleas.

In a number of lament psalms, the speaker takes comfort in thinking about God's power in creation; by implication he is reassuring himself that the God who created everything has the power to save him. So, for example, the psalmist in Psalm 77 reflects:

You are the God who works wonders . . .
When the waters saw you, they were afraid . . .
The clouds poured out water . . .
The crash of your thunder was in the whirlwind . . .
Your way was through the sea . . . (vv. 14-19)

And the speaker of Psalm 102 proclaims, "Long ago you laid the foundation of the earth, and the heavens are the work of your hands" (v. 25). In the book of Job, it is God who, when he finally shows his face and speaks to Job (chap. 38), reminds him of God's creative power. The passage functions like the ones in the psalms; it serves to remind Job that his situation is not hopeless because God is not helpless. God who tamed the Behemoth and Leviathan (chaps. 40 and 41) can also overcome the evil that Job suffers.

There are so many parallels between these psalms of lament and the speeches of Job, it is hard to know whether Job is intentionally quoting or alluding to them or is simply tapping into the psyche of a people covenanted to God, who are bewildered to find themselves defeated by an enemy and exiled from their home. But in a couple of instances, it is clear that Job is deliberately parodying a psalm that expresses trust in God's goodness. The first of these occurs in chapter 7, where Job twists the tenor and meaning of Psalm 8. Psalm 8 is full of wonder and praise for God's concern for human beings:

> When I look at your heavens, the work of your fingers,
>> the moon and the stars that you have established;
> what are human beings that you are mindful of them,
>> mortals that you care for them?
>
> Yet you have made them a little lower than God,
>> and crowned them with glory and honor. (vv. 3-5)[5]

Job turns that into sarcasm:

> What are human beings, that you make much of them,
>> that you set your mind on them? . . .
> Will you not look away from me for a while,
>> let me alone until I swallow my spittle?
> If I sin, what do I do to you, you watcher of humanity? (7:17-20)

---

5. The phrase now translated "human beings" and "mortals" is *ben 'adam* in Hebrew, which means "son of Adam"—that is, "son of man" or human being. I prefer this translation because I think it lies behind Christ's self-reference as "son of man."

Three chapters later, Job plays with the same theme of God's closeness to human beings. In Psalm 139 the speaker expresses gratitude for God's intimate involvement in his life:

> O LORD, you have searched me and known me.
> You know when I sit down and when I rise up . . .
>   you knit me together in my mother's womb.
> I praise you, for I am fearfully and wonderfully made.
>   Wonderful are your works. (vv. 1-2; 13b-14)

Job in his despair, however, sees God in almost opposite terms:

> Your hands fashioned and made me;
>   and now you turn and destroy me.
> Remember that you fashioned me like clay;
>   and will you turn me to dust again? (10:8-9)

Both Job and the Psalms are difficult to date, but the parallels and parodies make it reasonable to suppose that the book of Job came after a number of the psalms and that the author consciously drew on them to express the feelings of one who suffers evil in spite of his own faithfulness to God and to goodness. As in the psalms, Job's lament is expressed in the first person but could well represent the exiled Israelite community trying to understand how God could have allowed it to suffer so much loss.

To the extent that Job's pain may be seen as paradigmatic of Israel's history, it is not surprising to find parallels as well between Job and both Jeremiah and Isaiah. Job's cursing of the day he was born, for example, is similar to that of Jeremiah. In chapter 3, Job laments his birth: "Let the day perish in which I was born, and the night that said, 'A man-child is conceived'" (3:3). In similar terms, Jeremiah cries out: "Cursed be the day on which I was born! The day when my mother bore me, let it not be blessed! Cursed be the man who brought the news to my father, saying, 'A child is born to you, a son'" (20:14-15). Job and Jeremiah also both complain about violence being done against them. Job protests to God, "Even when I cry out 'Violence!' I am not answered" (19:7a).

In different language but with similar emotion, Jeremiah says, "For I hear the many whispering: 'Terror is all around! Denounce him! Let us denounce him!'" (20:10). In terms of his general or paradigmatic situation, Job is not unlike Isaiah's Suffering Servant, the righteous man whose marred appearance causes him to be "despised and rejected by others" (Isa 53:3) but whose suffering is undeserved. Both the Servant and Job speak about being spit upon (Isa 50:6b; Job 30:10). Yet Isaiah's Servant never complains about his fate, while Job protests his innocence again and again.

In fact, it is Job's refusal to accept his situation that constitutes the meat of the book and the essence of his faith. Job faces head-on the conventional pieties about human suffering (conventional as much now as then): if God is both all-powerful and all-good, then human beings who suffer must deserve it. The inverse of the argument is that if the innocent suffer, then God is either not all-powerful or not all-good. Job, however, refuses to accept the seeming logic of this syllogism. He insists that, contradictory as it may seem, all three things are true: God is good, God is in charge, and Job is innocent. He does not try to explain how this can be; in fact, much of his lament is asking why. Yet he never wavers in his faith in a caring God. Most remarkable of all, he believes that he will see God's face and that God will speak to him. This idea of God is not shared by the other figures in the narrative who, in various ways, suggest that God is distant from human beings and far too remote to talk with them.

If one focuses solely on the contentions of Job's would-be comforters, the book of Job presents a seemingly endless repetition of dreary insistence that everyone deserves what he or she gets. But if one considers the larger narrative, one sees that when God finally does appear and speaks to Job, then Job's idea of God is vindicated, just as Job predicted. When God appears, he says to Eliphaz: "My wrath is kindled against you and your two friends; for you have not spoken of me what is right, as my servant Job has" (42:7). So, first appearances to the contrary, the book of Job, like the lament psalm, does contain a dramatic movement and an intervention of grace.

It is the elements of that drama I would like to consider next, for it seems to me they represent a shift—even an evolution—in human understanding of God. In particular, I would argue that the work as a whole, through its many and varying arguments about God, moves from seeing God as distant from human beings to knowing God as close and intimately involved in human life.

The prose opening imagines God as emotionally detached from human life. God may boast of Job's faithfulness but is so distanced from Job's well-being that God is willing to place a wager on Job's happiness. The arguments of Job's friends also stress God's remoteness from human feeling. Eliphaz, the first among them to speak, expresses the conventional wisdom that good people prosper while evil ones suffer:

> Think now, who that was innocent ever perished?
>   Or where were the upright cut off?
> As I have seen, those who plow iniquity
>   and sow trouble reap the same.
> By the breath of God they perish. (4:7-9)

It is the same wisdom that is expressed throughout Proverbs and in Psalm 1, among other places. And it is hardly out of date: how many today, consciously or subconsciously, believe that if they are prosperous, they have earned it, while those who are miserable must have brought it on themselves?

Bildad, the second comforter, continues the argument by stressing God's justice:

> Does God pervert justice?
>   Or does the Almighty pervert the right?
> If your children sinned against him
>   he delivered them into the power of their transgression. (8:3-4)

Zophar, the third friend to speak, assures Job that his demand for intimacy with God is wishful thinking and an act of hubris:

> Can you find out the deep things of God?
>> Can you find out the limit of the Almighty?
> It is higher than heaven—what can you do?
>> Deeper than Sheol—what can you know? (11:7-8)

Zophar urges Job simply to change his misfortune by changing himself: "If iniquity is in your hand, put it far away. . . .You will lie down, and no one will make you afraid" (11:14, 19).

Job, however, will not accept this solution because he knows he does not deserve his pain. So he rejects Zophar's advice as insulting and beside the point:

> What you know, I also know;
>> I am not inferior to you.
> But I would speak to the Almighty,
>> and I desire to argue my case with God. (13:2-3)

That insistence on arguing with God—and the belief that God does talk with human beings—is the core of Job's faith. Job clings to this view of God's relationship with him, no matter what—even though God should "slay" him, even if others see him as impious:

> See, he will kill me; I have no hope;
>> But I will defend my ways to his face.
> This will be my salvation,
>> that the godless shall not come before him. (13:15-16)

It is a bold assertion. Even further, Job imagines what a dialogue with God might be like; he assumes God's love for him:

> You would call, and I would answer you.
>> you would long for the work of your hands.
> For then you would not number my steps,
>> you would not keep watch over my sin;
> my transgression would be sealed up in a bag,
>> and you would cover over my iniquity. (14:15-17)

Eliphaz finds Job's vision unacceptable: "But you are doing away with the fear of God. . . . Your own mouth condemns you, and not I" (15:4, 6). His perspective sends Job back to despair, and he not only speaks of his "miserable comforters" (16:2) but he sees God also as his enemy: "God gives me up to the ungodly, and casts me into the hands of the wicked" (16:11). Bildad and Job then exchange accusations. Bildad begins, "How long will you hunt for words? . . .Why are we counted as cattle?" (18:2-3), and Job retorts, "How long will you torment me, and break me in pieces with words?" (19:2). In Job's eyes, the torment of his supposed friends melds with God's attitude towards him:

> He breaks me down on every side, and I am gone,
>   he has uprooted my hope like a tree.
> He has kindled his wrath against me,
>   and counts me as his adversary. (19:10-11)

Job then recounts his alienation from family, close friends, servants, even his wife and young children (19:13-18), and everyone he is closest to:

> All my intimate friends abhor me,
>   and those whom I loved have turned against me.
> My bones cling to my skin and to my flesh,
>   and I have escaped by the skin of my teeth. (19:19-20)

His cry for help that follows seems to appeal to friends that no longer exist:

> Have pity on me, have pity on me, O you my friends,
>   for the hand of God has touched me! (19:21)

Yet at that very lowest point of complete abandonment, Job utters his greatest act of faith: "For I know that my Vindicator lives . . . and after my skin has been thus destroyed, then in my flesh I shall see God" (19:25-26).

Nineteen chapters later, Job's faith is vindicated, and he does see God. He not only sees God but also hears him and speaks with him. This dialogue with God—not the numerical restoration of possessions and children—is Job's real reward. His projected intimacy with God is realized.

It is fascinating to see how Job's understanding of God, versus that of other figures in the story, seems to be reflected in the names for God that appear throughout the narrative.

The narrative alternates between calling God *Elohim* and *Yahweh*—the two chief names for God in the Hebrew Bible. Elohim is plural in form, singular in Jewish understanding. Outside of Judaism, the plural form is used to refer to a whole range of gods, such as were found among the Canaanites; within Judaism, it is understood to refer to the one God of Israel. Mark Smith has suggested that this grammatical oddity may imply an evolution in Jewish thinking, a gradual growth towards monotheism.[6] Yahweh is the most common way that God is referred to in the Hebrew Bible, but it is not actually a name in itself; it is composed of the initial letters of the phrase God uses to respond to Moses' request for God's name: "I am who I am" or "I will be who I will be" (Exod 3:14). (The verb "to be" in Hebrew is not restricted to a particular tense.)

The name Elohim is associated with different traits of God than those connected to Yahweh. Although generalizations are always tricky, one might say that Elohim is more remote from human beings than Yahweh, not speaking to them directly but only through dreams and messengers, while Yahweh is given to entering into immediate and intimate dialogue. These observable differences gave rise to the theory that the Pentateuch had two (or more) different authors, each given to a different concept of God.[7] The author of Job is of course not proposing or following a critical theory, but

6. Mark Smith, *God in Translation: Deities in Cross-Cultural Discourse in the Biblical World* (Tübingen: Mohr Siebeck, 2008), 19.

7. In the late nineteenth century, Julius Wellhausen proposed four different authors. His theory, known as the Documentary Hypothesis, was articulated

throughout his work he does seem to be playing with the different ideas of God that had surfaced in Jewish texts.

In the description of Job as "a man who feared God" (1:1), the name for God appears as Elohim. Again the name for God is Elohim when the author tells us that Job offered extra sacrifices to God on behalf of his children, just in case one of them had sinned (1:5). Yet when the author recounts the wager between God and "the satan," an interesting thing happens: "the satan" (that is, "the adversary," not the devil of the New Testament) continues to refer to God as Elohim, but the author speaks of Yahweh. When the chapter concludes with Job's first great profession of faith—the words that have continued in Jewish tradition as its sacred *kaddish*, a prayer that blesses God in time of death and mourning—the word for God is Yahweh: "*Yahweh* gives and *Yahweh* takes away. Blessed be the name of *Yahweh*" (1:21). It seems to be a name for God consciously chosen to express faith, even in time of loss, in God's caring relationship with human beings.

Job's wife uses Elohim when she tells Job to "curse God and die" (2:10), and the three "comforters" routinely use El or Elohim, and occasionally *Shaddai* (the Almighty). Elihu, as well, who basically repeats the arguments of the first three (chaps. 32–37), also uses Elohim as his name for God. Job himself seems affected by this nomenclature and, after his initial expression of trust in Yahweh, uses some form of Elohim when he curses the day he was born (3:4), speaks of the "terrors of God" (6:4), demands that God tell him why God is crushing him (10:2-3), asserts he would like to argue with God (13:30), and even when he proclaims, "I shall see God" (19:26).

Yet when God answers Job, it is Yahweh who speaks (38:1; 40:3, 6). And when Job speaks back to God—as he had longed desired—he speaks to Yahweh (42:1). And, in fact, in the whole last chapter, "Yahweh" is the only word for God. When God reprimands

---

in his *Prolegomena to the History of Ancient Israel* (1882), and it dominated much of twentieth-century biblical work. It has been challenged in recent times.

Eliphaz and his friends for not speaking rightly about God the way Job has, it is Yahweh who is angry (42:7-8). And when the three comply, it is to Yahweh that they respond (42:9). When God regards "the face of Job" (42:9), it is Yahweh who is gazing at him. And it is Yahweh who turns around (the word is *shuv*) the "captivity" of Job, restores all he had lost (42:10), and "blessed the last days of Job more than the beginning" (42:12).

Since both the opening and closing chapters of the book of Job are in prose while the rest are in verse, it is common to contrast the prose frame with the poetic middle. The frame offers a simplistic story of a blameless man who lost everything he had in life and then regained it. At first glance, readers are rightly repelled by the idea that being given a second "set" of children would compensate for losing the first batch. But a closer look at the book of Job shows that it is much more complex than that. It has several overlapping structures that work simultaneously. The most obvious is the prose frame, which indeed seems to read like a simple folktale. A second is the structure of the lament psalm, which begins in despair and ends in blessing. Like many such psalms, it is filled with varying, and even seesawing, emotions before a cry for help, a proclamation of faith, and a happy ending. But even more significant is the slowly evolving idea of God, reflected in the subtle shifts between Elohim and Yahweh. "The satan," the three comforters, Job's wife, and Elihu all base their arguments against Job on their idea of God as a remote deity, too distant from human beings to listen to them or talk with them. Only Job sees God as one in dialogue with human beings—not Elohim, but Yahweh. At the end, Job's well-being is restored not by possessions and children but by Yahweh's assurance that his understanding of God is the right one. The book of Job offers for contemplation an evolution in human understanding of the relationship between the human and the divine.

In this regard, it is not insignificant that God answers Job *out of* the storm, not above it. God is not remote from what is happening; God is at the center. As in Exodus 3:7-8, God has heard

Job's cry, knows his sufferings, and has come to deliver him. God was not the cause of Job's anguish, but in speaking to him, God becomes his redeemer. "Where is [God] the father?" "The father" is right here talking to Job.

God's talk largely takes the form of stern rebuke. At first, God's questions to Job seem designed to overpower him: "Where were you when I laid the foundation of the earth?" (38:4); "Have you commanded the morning?" (38:12); "Have you entered into the springs of the sea?" (38:16); "Have the gates of death been revealed to you?" (38:17). Yet amid these images of sheer power are ones that indicate the full richness of God's being. God speaks of "when the morning stars sang together" (38:7), revealing God's embrace of beauty and joy. And God expresses tender concern for vulnerable creatures: "Who provides for the raven its prey, when its young ones cry to God, and wander about for lack of food?" (38:41). In any case, what matters most is that God has heard Job, has listened to him, and has come to respond to him. It is particularly in that sense that God is acting as the father that Jewish texts proclaim in both prophecy and prayer.[8]

To assess the effect of God's speech on Job, we must take into account both Job's words and his actions. At first glance, his words seem self-debasing: "See, I am of small account; what shall I answer you? I lay my hand on my mouth" (40:4). Yet silence is the response of awe. What is more, even as Job proclaims his silence,

---

8. In the middle of the twentieth century, a German scholar, Joachim Jeremias, proposed, in the first chapter of his book, *The Central Meaning of the New Testament* (New York: Charles Scribner, 1965), the theory that Jesus' invocation of God as "Abba" showed that he had a special intimacy with God hitherto unknown. Great scholar that he was, it is surprising that Jeremias did not realize that "Abba" did not mean "Daddy," as he said, but was simply the Aramaic form of "father." Later scholarship has shown the close relationship between Jesus' "Our Father" and many prayers in ancient Jewish liturgy. See *The Lord's Prayer and Jewish Liturgy*, ed. Jakob J. Petuchowski and Michael Brocke (New York: Seabury Press, 1978).

he goes on talking: "I have spoken once, and I will not answer; twice, but will proceed no further" (40:5). And when Job in fact does go on to speak again, his tone has the relaxed quality of one who is speaking to a friend. If Job felt truly overpowered by God, he would not be talking at all. But Job not only speaks but also echoes once again Psalm 139, only this time he says it straight, without any sarcastic overtones: "Therefore I have uttered what I did not understand, things too wonderful for me" (42:3). The psalmist in Psalm 139 says, "Such knowledge is too wonderful for me" (v. 6), because he is overcome by God's intimate knowledge of him. Job seems to be expressing the same feeling when he makes a distinction between hearing and seeing God—that is, between intellectual knowledge of God and direct experience. And although his final description of himself as "dust and ashes" (42:6) may seem to be totally self-effacing, it is well to remember that they echo Abraham's words even as he launched into his great argument with God over Sodom (Gen 18:27). The Jewish argument with God, so spiritedly engaged in by Abraham, is continued in Job's bold (and rewarded) demands.

Job's actions confirm that his encounter with God has changed him. He now relates to his children differently than he did before. His new relationship with Yahweh makes him more confident in God's blessing, more joyful about life. So he no longer offers extra sacrifices, as though he needed to appease a wrathful deity. And he gives his daughters wildly fond and frivolous names: Dove, Cinnamon, and Horn of Eye-Shadow.[9] And finally, with a doting generosity beyond the law, he bestows on them a legacy equal to that of their brothers.

9. This translation of names is taken from Ellen Davis, "Job and Jacob: The Integrity of Faith," in *Reading Between the Texts: Intertextuality and the Hebrew Bible*, edited by Danna Nolan Fewell (Louisville, KY: Westminster Press, 1992), 203–24.

In the book of Job, God evolves from a distant deity into a caring father. And Job evolves from a worried observer of God's law into a playful and loving image of Yahweh.

It may be worth observing that these dramatic shifts do not represent an evolution in the sense of humankind progressing for all time from one understanding of God to another. On the contrary, it is clear that both concepts of the divine are still around; human beings, if they acknowledge a deity at all, move between them both. But the book of Job offers evidence of the way evolution works in theology as well as in nature: not in one direction only, but in several at once. For the author of Job, the idea of a distant deity who lays down strict laws and then punishes those who break them is both primitive and impoverished. Through the drama of Job, he sets forth his vision of a divine being who is close enough to human beings to engage them in a conversation.

The Changing God of Job

The book of Job dramatizes the observation of Teilhard that heads this chapter: "All around us, and within our own selves, God is in the process of 'changing,' as a result of the coincidence of his magnetic power and our own Thought." Or, as Teilhard also says, "God in some way 'transforms' himself as he incorporates us. . . . We have to do more to disclose Him (or even, in one sense of the word, 'complete' Him) and ever more fully."[10] The dialogues between Job and his comforters wrestle with the question of God's relationship to suffering human beings. The comforters articulate the primitive perception of an impersonal, angry god, while Job insists on a caring and intimate God. In the end, the author dramatizes the validity of Job's perspective. In the process, the human idea of God changes before our eyes. Job's faith in some way "transforms" and "completes" God, even as God "incorporates" Job

10. *Heart of Matter*, 54.

and transforms him into a clearer reflection of a compassionate divine Being. Job's suffering itself paradoxically draws him forward into a more joyful, light-hearted existence.

The deity who transforms Job cannot be boxed in by any human definition. Rather, this divine being is one who draws humanity forward into new and unimagined states of consciousness. The action of Job's story translates YHWH into its ultimate meaning: "I will be who I will be." It is in sync with Teilhard's prayerful reflection, "You [Lord] have become for my mind and heart much more than He who was and who is; you have become *He who shall be*."[11]

---

11. *Heart of Matter*, 56.

2

Ascent, Secrets, Ecstasy
Metaphors for
Expanding Consciousness

> "Zoologically and psychologically speaking, the
> Human Being can at last be seen in the cosmic
> integrity of his trajectory, on which, however, he
> is still at only an embryonic stage—if we look
> ahead we can already see the outlines of a wide
> fringe of ULTRA-HUMAN."[1]

Job's longing to see God's face, his insistence on
confronting God directly, is not an anomaly in Jewish
texts but an essential element in Jewish tradition. In
the book of Job this human desire is expressed through
the literary forms of lament and dialogue. In other
Jewish texts, it is expressed through mystical images,
often connected to Ezekiel's vision of God's throne or
chariot. Gershom Sholem, in his book *Major Trends
in Jewish Mysticism*, suggests three prevailing themes
in mystical literature: ascent, secrets, and ecstasy.[2] Each
of these has its corresponding set of imagery.

1. Teilhard de Chardin, *The Heart of Matter*, 38.
2. New York: Schocken Books, 1941; repr. 1973.

The image of physical ascent beyond the earth through the heavens symbolizes the soul's expansion beyond the confines of its immediate space into another dimension of reality. In this state of spiritual transcendence, the person is given to understand the cosmos in a fuller way, along with his or her own place in it; these are the "secrets" or mysteries of revelation. This revelation has a powerful effect on those who receive it: they are emotionally and mentally blown away; they become *ek-static*—that is, they are shaken out of their normal, humdrum states of mind into a new consciousness. Revelation transforms them.

The book of Job is related to this mystical path, even though in Job's case it is suffering that first jostles him out of his routine ways. His demand that God speak with him is nonetheless a demand for transcendence, and his face-to-face encounter with God involves both a revelation and a transformation. What is revealed to Job is the grandeur of the universe; what he grasps, paradoxically, is both his smallness and his significance. Job comes away from this experience a different man.

Similarly, the prophets also encounter God directly and are forever changed. Moses, like Job, talks with God face-to-face and comes away with a mission (Exod 3:3-10). Isaiah's mouth is touched with burning coal (Isa 6:6-7), and he has visions of "the earth full of the knowledge of the LORD" (Isa 11:9). The Lord touches Jeremiah's mouth and puts his own words into it (Jer 1:9). And Ezekiel has a mystical encounter in which God's throne is glorious almost beyond description. Ezekiel is simply "son of man" or "son of Adam"—a mere mortal called to witness to God's majesty (Ezek 1:1-2), yet God opens Ezekiel's mouth so he can eat the scroll of God's wisdom (3:1-3). Although Judaism formally distinguishes the writings of the Prophets from the Wisdom writings of the sages, there is continuity in the wisdom of Israel: all of it is aimed at showing the transformative effect on human beings when they come to share in the divine perspective.

Just before and after the time of the gospels, a body of mystical writings appeared in Judaism that particularly utilized the metaphors of ascent, secrets, and ecstasy. Alternately designated Jewish or Christian, they dramatize some biblical figure ascending through the heavens where he is first given to understand the secrets of the cosmos and is then transformed into a heavenly figure. Although these writings were never taken into either the Christian or Jewish canons of the fourth and fifth centuries, they formed an important part of the religious landscape of the first century. They are significant in two ways. First, they show how deeply the mystical elements of the Christian narrative are rooted in Jewish mysticism. Second, they provide ancient evidence of the human experience of expanded consciousness.

Martha Himmelfarb, writing about eight examples of this literature, notes:

> The claim that a human being can become the equal of angels stands at the center of early Jewish and Christian apocalypses in which ascent to heaven is the mode of revelation.[3]

> The apocalypses with transformation of men into angels belong to one strand of a large and diverse body of literature that treats the biblical patriarchs and especially Moses as in some sense divine.[4]

Her study includes the two halves of First Enoch—the Book of Watchers (chaps. 1–36) and the Similitudes (chaps. 37–71)—Second Enoch, the Testament of Levi, the Apocalypse of Zephaniah, the Apocalypse of Abraham, the Ascension of Isaiah, and Third Baruch.

These ascensions of human beings are sometimes called "apocalypses" because cosmic secrets are uncovered or revealed through

---

3. Martha Himmelfarb, *Ascent to Heaven in Jewish and Christian Apocalypses* (New York: Oxford University Press, 1993), 3.

4. Himmelfarb, *Ascent to Heaven*, 48.

the process of ascent. The underlying assumption of these works is that on earth, God's truth is always hidden. To discover it—or *uncover* it (which "apocalypse" literally means)—requires a desire for God, symbolized by the image of ascent, and self-forgetfulness, symbolized by the image of ecstasy, the soul outside or beside itself, delighting in the Other.

In this chapter I would like to look at one particular example— the spiritual transformation of Enoch, especially as it is described in the earliest Enoch narrative (dated anywhere between the second century BCE and the first century CE). Enoch is a biblical figure who does not die. The biblical account is sparse and mysterious: "Enoch walked with God; then he was no more, because God took him" (Gen 5:24).

No one is quite sure what that last statement means, but its ambiguity has opened the door to mystical interpretations. The earliest of these, known as 1 Enoch or the Ethiopian Apocalypse of Enoch, imagines Enoch ascending through seven heavens. On the way he has a series of visions, mostly about the final judgment of both human beings and angels, but also of God's palace and throne—a vision that owes much to Ezekiel. Afterwards, "spiritual beings" show him the secrets of the cosmos:

> And they took me into a place of whirlwind in the mountain; the top of its summit was reaching into heaven. . . . And I saw chambers of light and thunder. . . . And they lifted me up unto the waters of life. . . . I saw all the great rivers and reached to the great darkness and went into the place where all flesh must walk cautiously [or, where no flesh can walk]. (17:2-7)

> And I saw storerooms of all the winds and how with them he has embroidered all creation as well as the foundations of the earth. I saw the cornerstone of the earth; I saw the four winds which bear the earth as well as the firmament of heaven. . . . I saw the souls carried by the clouds. I saw

the path of angels in the ultimate end of the earth.
(18:1-5)[5]

Enoch is finally taken to "the garden of righteousness" and "the
tree of wisdom"—the tree of Adam and Eve (32:6). From there he
journeys "to the extreme ends of the earth" (33:1) and comes to see
"the gates of heaven" (33–36). In the second book of the work,
known as the "Similitudes" or "Parables," Enoch's understanding
of the "mysteries" of the universe is deepened. He gains insight into
Wisdom herself: "Wisdom could not find a place in which she
could dwell but a place was found for her in the heavens" (42:1).

Enoch's remarkable journey concludes with a vision of a figure
who existed "before time" and who is called either "the son of man"
or "the son of human beings."

> At that place I saw one to whom belongs the time before
> time. And his head was white as wool. . . . "This is the son
> of man [or, the son of human beings], to whom belongs
> righteousness, and with whom righteousness dwells. And
> he will open all the hidden storerooms; for the Lord of
> Spirits has chosen him, and he is destined to be victorious
> before the Lord of Spirits in eternal uprightness." (46:1-4)

> Furthermore, I saw in that place the fountain of righteous-
> ness. . . . All the thirsty ones drink and become filled with
> wisdom. . . . At that hour, the son of man was given a name
> [or, the sons of men were named by a name]. . . . He is the
> light of the gentiles and he will become the hope of those
> who are sick in their hearts. All those who dwell on earth
> shall fall and worship before him; they shall glorify, bless, and
> sing the name of the Lord of Spirits. For this purpose he
> became the Chosen One; he was concealed in the presence

---

5. All translations of the Enoch literature are taken from *The Old Testament Pseudepigrapha*, ed. James H. Charlesworth, vol. 1 (Garden City, NY:
Doubleday, 1983).

of (the Lord of Spirits) prior to the creation of the world,
and for eternity. And he has revealed the wisdom of the Lord
of Spirits to the righteous and the holy ones. (48:1-7)

There are many elements in this work that are repeated in the
gospel narratives. First of all, there is the intriguing figure called
"son of man," Jesus' most common way of referring to himself in
the gospels. The desire to connect this figure with Christ is evident
in the work of E. Isaac, who translated the work into English in
James Charlesworth's edition of *The Old Testament Pseudepigrapha*.
He capitalizes the phrase so as to turn it into a title. Then he acknowledges in a footnote that he did not translate it exactly the
way it reads. He says, "'Man' in this context means 'people' or
'human beings.' Though this passage could be rendered 'Son of
human beings,' to avoid unnecessary confusion, I have used 'Son
of Man,' which has become an accepted and standard expression
among scholars for a long time."[6] Of course, his well-intentioned
modification of the original has only added to the confusion about
what "son of man" means in any text. I would argue that, in this
case, the Enoch narrative is so clearly indebted to Ezekiel that the
phrase must be understood to mean what it does there—simply
human being (*ben 'adam*). This reading is confirmed, I think, later
in the book when Enoch himself is addressed by an angel as "son
of man." Such an understanding does not disconnect the phrase
from the gospels but instead gives support to those who see Jesus'
self-reference as a way of emphasizing that he is like the first
human being—as it were, a second Adam. This emphasis, in turn,
does not detract from his being "son of God" as well; it simply
points to the conjunction of humanity with divinity.

The reader will also be reminded, of course, of the vision in
Daniel where Daniel sees the "son of man" (NAB) or "one like a
human being" (NRSV) coming on heavenly clouds (Dan 7:13).
The controversy over the meaning of the phrase (is this a divine

6. *Old Testament Pseudepigrapha*, 34n46e.

title or a generic description?) is reflected in the footnotes. The NRSV note on "one like a human being" informs us: "This figure represents the faithful Jews and should probably be identified with the archangel Michael, although he was traditionally associated with the messiah." The NAB note puts it somewhat differently, saying that Jesus "made the title, 'Son of Man,' his most characteristic way of referring to himself, as the One in whom and through whom the salvation of God's people came to be realized." Both explanations suggest that angelic figures may take on human appearance, and vice versa. It also suggests that in that time period, the border between human and angelic (divine or semi-divine) was fluid and porous.

There are other phrases in Enoch's description of this human figure that catch the attention of the Christian reader: namely, that he is "the light of the gentiles," that he is called "the chosen one," that he was preexistent, and that, for a long time, he was "concealed" by God. The "light of the gentiles" recalls Isaiah's description of Israel's vocation (Isa 42:6)—a phrase Luke shows Simeon applying to Jesus (Luke 2:32). The "chosen one" is a designation suggesting the messiah. The attribute of preexistence is applied to Jesus in the Gospel of John. The notion that Jesus' identity was hidden and secret is dramatized in the Gospel of Mark.

Perhaps most striking is the description of this figure as "the hope of those who are sick in their hearts," because it characterizes the messiah not as a victorious figure but as a healing one. One who gives hope to the heart-sick is not going to "restore the kingdom to Israel" (Acts 1:6) militarily or politically but in a spiritual way.

At the conclusion of this section, there is another last judgment scene in which those who are not saved are said to "have denied the Lord of the Spirits and his messiah" (48:10). This messiah is filled with the gifts of the Spirit:

> In him dwells the spirit of wisdom, the spirit which gives thoughtfulness, the spirit of knowledge and strength, the spirit of those who have fallen asleep in their righteousness. He shall judge the secret things. (49:3-4)

The passage bears an echo of Isaiah:

> The spirit of the LORD shall rest on him,
>   the spirit of wisdom and understanding,
>   the spirit of counsel and might,
>   the spirit of knowledge and fear of the LORD. (11:2)

Significantly, too, this "chosen one"—like the Christ of the gospels—has been raised from death by God. Interestingly, the passage that mentions this also quotes from Psalm 114, one of the *hallel* psalms recited or sung at Passover, thus setting this messiah's resurrection, as the gospels do, in a Passover context:

> In those days, mountains shall dance like rams; and the hills shall leap like kids satiated with milk [Ps. 114:4]. And the faces of all the angels in heaven shall glow with joy because on that day, the Elect One has arisen. (51:4)

Enoch's visions continue through the remaining chapters. In chapter 70, he describes his own departure from the earth:

> And it happened after this that his [Enoch's] living name was raised up before the son of man and to the Lord from among those who dwell on earth. It was lifted up in a wind [or spirit] chariot and it disappeared from among them. From that day on, I was not counted among them. But he placed me between two winds. . . . And there I saw the first (human) ancestors and the righteous ones of old, dwelling in that place. (70:1-4)

Enoch leaves the earth much as Elijah did, in a heavenly chariot (2 Kgs 2:11). What is more, he envisions some form of heavenly dwelling where he will meet his ancestors—a form of immortality not imagined in the Bible. More "secrets" or mysteries are revealed to him: he has a vision of "the secrets of mercy" along with "the secrets of righteousness" and "the secrets of the extreme ends of heaven" (71:4).

Once again, he sees "the Antecedent of Time," whose head is described (as in Dan 7:9) as being white and "pure like wool" and whose garment is "indescribable" (71:10-11). Enoch is overwhelmed: "I fell on my face, my whole body mollified and my spirit transformed" (71:11).

In general, the reader is struck by the elements that indicate how Enoch has transcended conventional human limits. First of all, one notices how the drama of human ascent through the heavens breaks through the normal boundaries of space. Second, one is struck by the presence of someone called "the Antecedent of Time"—that is, by one who disrupts the conventional sequencing of events and whose head, being "white as wool" (71:10), suggests an angelic figure. Accompanying these startling upsets of space and time, and the presence of a semidivine figure, is Enoch's new perspective on the cosmos, particularly a deeper insight into winds and water and sun. This shift in understanding is brought about by angelic intermediaries between the human and divine. The climax is an experience so overwhelming that Enoch responds by falling on his face—a posture expressing awe. In a somewhat later version of the story (first century BCE to late first century CE), Enoch's own appearance is transformed; he exchanges "earthly garments" for glorious ones and his appearance is radiant:

> And the Lord said to Michael: Take Enoch and take off his earthly garments, and anoint [him] with good oil, and clothe [him] in glorious garments. . . . And the appearance of the oil [was] more [resplendent] than a great light, and its richness like a sweet dew, and its fragrance like myrrh. . . . And I looked at myself, and I was like one of the glorious ones, and there was no apparent difference. (9:17-19)

If these events were couched in modern English instead of in ancient Ethiopic, Aramaic, Greek, and Slavonic, we might think we were reading modern science fiction. Conventional understandings of space and time are shaken up. The secrets of the earth reside in the primordial sources of energy—wind, water, and sun. The division between the human and the divine is blurred by angelic creatures who seem to have the characteristics of both. The central human figure seems to shift from one realm to the other. The key question of later Christian theology also seems to be anticipated here: Is this figure human or divine?

The "Ultra-Human" in the Gospels, in the Enoch Narratives, and in Teilhard

In the gospels, many of the same mystical elements that characterize the Enoch narratives appear in the scenes where Christ transcends ordinary human limits: his ascension into heaven, his resurrection from the dead, and, above all, his transfiguration. The church has separated these events into three discrete liturgical moments, but essentially they represent one and the same human movement towards the divine sphere.

In the Gospel of John, Jesus appears as one transfigured—that is, divine—from the opening words of the Prologue. Jesus is antecedent to time: "in the beginning with God" (1:3). He is "the light of all people" and "the light that shines in the darkness" (1:4-5). He proclaims his oneness with God throughout the narrative. In the conclusion of his gospel, John indicates that Jesus' appearance shifted after his resurrection: Mary mistakes him for the gardener. The same ambiguity about how Jesus is perceived also occurs in Luke 24, where the disciples on the road to Emmaus fail to recognize Jesus until their memory is jogged by his breaking of the bread. Both Luke and John seem to suggest that while Christ partakes of divinity from the beginning, he begins to have the appearance of divinity only after his resurrection. Further, John indicates that this shift is a process: "Do not hold on to me," he tells Mary, "because I have not yet ascended to the Father" (20:17).

In the Synoptic narratives, the first glimpse of Christ ascending towards heaven takes the form of his going up a mountain (Mark 9:2; Matt 17:3; Luke 9:28), an echo, of course, of Moses ascending to Sinai. The heavenly guides or intermediaries are the two great prophets, Moses and Elijah, who seem to appear outside of history. They are timeless, symbolic figures, existing, it seems, in their ascended state of being. Jesus is transfigured before his disciples in a way that echoes "the Antecedent One" in his whiteness and Second Enoch in his glorious radiance. Mark says that "his garments became dazzling white, such as no one on earth could bleach them" (9:3). Matthew says that "his face shone like the sun, and his clothes became dazzling white" (17:2). Luke says that "the appearance of his face changed, and his clothes became dazzling white" (9:29).

Beholding this altered appearance, the disciples come to realize Jesus' divinity, and, recognizing it, they are overcome—like Enoch—with the holy fear that can also be described as overwhelming awe. Their sense of the *mysterium tremendum* makes them want to worship (Mark 9:5-6; Matt 17:4; Luke 9:33). In Mark and Luke this feeling of awe occurs at the sight of Jesus' transfigured body. In Matthew it occurs after the voice from heaven proclaims Jesus to be God's "beloved son" (17:5-6). In each case, we are told, the disciples—like Enoch—"fell on their faces and were filled with awe." The cosmic secret that has been revealed to them is the divinity of the one who calls himself "the son of man."

Typical of his fondness for doublets, Mark repeats this experience at the very end of his gospel. The three women who find the empty tomb, and who hear an angelic voice assure them that "he is risen," are possessed by "ecstasy" (the Greek word is *ekstasis*)—that is, they are stunned out of their normal understanding of human death and shocked into a new awareness of human possibility. Overwhelmed, as the disciples were, by their realization of Jesus' divinity, they fall silent just as the disciples did and remain speechless because "they were filled with awe." (The words are exactly the same as at the transfiguration.)

Translators of Mark's gospel have been deaf to Mark's choice of word here, turning *ekstasis* into "amazement" (KJV; NRSV) or "bewilderment" (NAB). But cultural history and biblical precedent, as well as the patterns of Mark's artistry, prove them insensitive.

Ecstasy is not a rare or bizarre phenomenon in the ancient world but, as Sholem has noted, a key element in Jewish mystical experience.[7] Within the Bible it appears more than once, and always in connection with some life-changing revelation. When Samuel first anoints Saul to be king, he tells him to expect certain signs that God has chosen him. Among them, he says, "[Y]ou will encounter a band of prophets . . . speaking in ecstasy" (1 Sam 10: 5; JSB). Samuel connects this experience to a change in Saul himself: "The spirit of the Lord will grip you, and you will speak in ecstasy along with them; you will become another man" (1 Sam 10:6).

The Septuagint—the Greek translation of the Hebrew Scriptures followed by the evangelists—uses the word "ecstasy" in Genesis as well. When God stuns the first human being so as to replace him with two, the Septuagint says God placed him in a state of *ekstasis* (Gen 2:21). Again, when God makes a covenant with Abraham, the Septuagint says God casts him into a state of *ekstasis* (Gen 15:12). In each case, the word indicates an expansion of human consciousness.

Mark clearly had this understanding of the word in mind when he chose to use it in his gospel at three key moments. When the crowd sees Jesus' cure of the paralytic, Mark says, "They were all ecstatic and glorified God, saying, 'We have never seen anything like this'" (2:12b). When Jesus brings Jairus's daughter back to life, Mark describes the reaction of the witnesses in similar terms, using the word in two different forms so that it literally reads, "They were out of their minds with ecstasy" (*exestēsan ekstasei*;

---

7. In addition, Karen Armstrong has repeatedly pointed to *ekstasis* as a religious mode in many religious traditions, expressing a "stepping outside" of the ego, a "transcendent dimension of life," and the culmination of revelation. See *A Case for God* (New York: Alfred A. Knopf, 2009), xiii, 10, 57, 63–64, 98–102. She links this mode to silence: "There is a long religious tradition that stressed the importance of recognizing the limits of our knowledge, of silence, of reticence, and awe" (xviii). Also see *The Great Transformation* (New York: Alfred A. Knopf, 2006), 61, 391, 393.

5:42b). The appearance of the word at the end of Mark's gospel is its third occurrence. Given Mark's well-known fondness for triads as a way to emphasize meaning, the reader should expect this third use to be significant.

Some translators may have been misled by the fact that *ekstasis* here is paired with "trembling." But if so, they have failed to notice that while Mark has earlier used the conventional phrase "fear and trembling" to describe the woman with the hemorrhage (5:33), he has carefully *not* used it here. Instead, he rearranges the order and places trembling first—a switch that should alert the reader to something different about to come. He then replaces the usual word for "fear" with "ecstasy." Still some translators may feel that ecstasy does not fit with the final verse, which they read to mean, "They said nothing to anyone because they were very much afraid" (16:8). But in fact, the phrase translated "very much afraid" should be rendered the way it is at the end of chapter 4, "filled with awe." (They are identical in Greek.) Moreover, the appearance here of *ekstasis* is Mark's clue that what he intends is not fear but *awe*, and the holy silence that accompanies human awareness of the *mysterium tremendum*. The women are silent here just as the disciples were silent before the revelation of Jesus' transfigured form. Through his choice of words Mark dramatizes, in both instances, an expansion of human consciousness—a new realization of the human potential to share in divinity.

The Enoch narratives dramatize the perception that human beings have the potential to be transformed into divine beings. The gospel narratives show us what it looks like when humanity and divinity cohere in one singular person. While each is distinctly different, they are both part of the same mystical apprehension that being human in some way involves becoming divine.

Evolution and the Metaphors for Expanding Consciousness

In our own time, Teilhard has called us to perceive that human evolution is not finished but is still drawing us forward to some kind of spiritual transformation. For Teilhard, this mystical perception is grounded in scientific fact. In the quote given at the head of the chapter, Teilhard observes that while the evolution of the human species "is still at only an embryonic stage," yet in terms of "the cosmic integrity" of its development, it can be seen moving towards the "ULTRA-HUMAN."

The Enoch narratives are one of the first pointers in this direction. The idea and image of ascent, which they dramatize so vividly, is integral to this perception. Teilhard uses this image to describe both his own growth and, more boldly, that of God:

"I managed to climb up to the point where the Universe became apparent to me as a great rising surge, in which all the work that goes into serious inquiry, all the will to create, all the acceptance of suffering, converge ahead into a single, dazzling spear-head—now, at the end of my life, I can stand on the peak I have scaled and continue to look ever more closely into the future, and there, with ever more assurance, see the ascent of God."[8]

8. *Heart of Matter*, 52.

3

From the Personification of Wisdom to the Person of Christ
The Evolving of the Divine Feminine

> "Every day supplies more irrefutable evidence
> that no man at all can dispense with the
> Feminine, any more than he can dispense with
> light, oxygen, or vitamins."[1]

The Mystical Implications
of God's Word in Judaism

In Proverbs 8:22-30, God's Word or Wisdom, for the first time in ancient Jewish texts, speaks for herself. As her personification develops, it evolves in two significant ways: she emerges as a symbol of the divine feminine; the ardent pursuit of her becomes a metaphor for the human seeking to complete itself with the divine.

Wisdom, first of all, is connected to the very beginning of creation. "Ages ago," she says, "I was set up, at the first, before the beginning of the earth" (v. 23). What does that mean—a moment before the earth exists? Here is Proverbs' literary vision:

1. Teilhard de Chardin, *The Heart of Matter*, 59.

When there were no depths I was brought forth,
   when there were no springs abounding with water.
Before the mountains had been shaped,
   before the hills, I was brought forth— . . .
When he established the heavens, I was there,
   when he drew a circle on the face of the deep, . . .
when he assigned to the sea its limit, . . .
   when he marked out the foundations of the earth. (vv. 24-29)

We are reminded of God spreading out before Job a glimpse of the first moments of existence:

Were you there when I laid the foundation of the earth? . . .
   Or who shut in the sea with doors
when it burst out from the womb? . . .
And said, "Thus far shall you come, and no farther,
   and here shall your proud waves be stopped?" (Job 38:4, 8, 11)

Seeing himself as part of the vast scheme of Creation brings Job to silence and the awe of God that is "the beginning of Wisdom." Here, the author of Proverbs envisions "the beginning of Wisdom" as the moment before all life began. Wisdom's claim is deeply provocative: "The LORD *begot /created* me the firstborn [or *beginning*] of his ways" (v. 22).[2]

The word translated "begot" is notably different from the word used in Genesis 1:1 to articulate God's creation of the heavens and the earth. At the same time, it is significantly the same as that

---

2. This is the NAB translation, the version used in the Catholic Lectionary. The verb here is a word whose meaning varies and is inferred from context; as such, it is open to multiple interpretations. English translations, both old and new, are of mixed minds. The King James Version reads, "The Lord *possessed* me in the beginning of his way." The NRSV, "The LORD *created* me *at* or *as* the beginning of his work." The JSB (*Jewish Study Bible*), ed. Adele Berlin and Marc Zvi Brettler (New York: Oxford University Press, 2004), "The Lord *created* me at the beginning of his course."

used in Psalm 139:13 to describe God's intimate involvement in the psalmist's conception: "You *formed* me in my mother's womb." The variations suggest the difference between something God makes at a distance and something into which God breathes God's own life. The verb indicates a creature that is not an object distinct from God but a part of God's very substance.

There are further implications that come from identifying Wisdom with *beginning*. James Kugel, in *The Bible as It Was*, spells out an unsuspected and fascinating meaning behind the use of this word.[3] He notes that early Jewish scholars of the Bible were perturbed by the opening of Genesis because the phrase we translate "In the beginning" literally means in Hebrew, "In the beginning *of*." Since the noun that follows is "God," the passage, if read literally, would suggest that God had a beginning. Searching Scripture to find another passage that would avoid the literal and illuminate the poetic meaning of this opening verse, scholars lit upon Proverbs 8:22, reading it to mean, "The Lord created (or begot) me *as the beginning* of his way." So, they concluded, "wisdom" and "beginning" are synonyms, and we should read the opening of Genesis to mean, "In *Wisdom* God created the heavens and the earth." They felt justified in doing this, Kugel says, because they held "the fundamental conviction that the Bible's precise wording is both utterly intentional . . . and infinitely significant."[4]

The Jewish Study Bible spells out further implications: "An important Jewish interpretation . . . uses Proverbs, chapter 8, to argue that the Torah (that is, the Bible, identified with Wisdom) was created before the world and was used by God in creating it" (1461).

Two Targums (early teaching translations of the Bible from Hebrew into Aramaic) reflect this understanding. The Fragment Targum reads, "*With Wisdom* did God create and perfect the

3. Cambridge, MA: Harvard University Press, 1997.
4. Kugel, *Bible as It Was*, 54–55.

heavens and the earth," and the Targum Neophyti, "In the begin-ning *with wisdom* did God create." And in general, Jewish tradition developed the idea that God's cultic creation—that is, the Torah—paralleled God's natural creation. This parallel, they argued, is evi-dent in Genesis 1 through its emphasis on God's Word or Wisdom as God's creative force: "God said, 'Let there be light,' and there was light" (Gen 1:3). Here God creates through Word alone.

In Jewish thought, God's creativity in the world of nature and the world of Scripture is perceived as parallel, and both are seen as re-vealing God's fecundity as ongoing and inexhaustible. Modern sci-ence has verified the idea of the unending activity of the universe in creating new species, new forms of being. Modern readings of Scrip-ture have verified the idea that human interpretation is never static but continues to shift with every generation. The latter has been particularly true in Jewish interpretation of Scripture, where God's ongoing creativity implies evolution in human understanding.

Michael Fishbane spells out how this works. He says that in the early centuries, religious Jews considered it "a religious task to re-actualize the sacred word for the present hour."[5] Fishbane con-siders the act of interpreting the biblical text to be itself a sacred act: "It partakes of the sanctity of Scripture even as it further re-veals it." By implication, he sees the whole Jewish Bible as sacred *interpretation*; in his view, interpretation is its overarching genre. He coined the phrase "inner-biblical exegesis" to describe this phenomenon.[6]

As Fishbane further describes it, this kind of exegesis involved the reappropriation of Scripture in different ways: sometimes through rewriting an original text, sometimes through juxtaposing discordant texts in order to create riddles and raise questions. It

5. *The Garments of Torah: Essays in Biblical Hermeneutics* (Bloomington: Indiana University Press, 1989), 38.

6. Initially an article in *Midrash and Literature*, ed. Geoffrey Hartman and Sanford Budick (New Haven, CT: Yale University Press, 1986), 19–37, it came to form the first chapter in *The Garments of Torah*.

involved constant allusions (explicit or implicit) to what was written before, a weaving together of many threads, using past language and imagery to interpret the present.

In some ways this playing with words and meanings may strike the reader as a game or a giant acrostic puzzle. But in Judaism, words have always had a mystical dimension. As the introduction to Hasidic prayer puts it:

> The glorification of the text of prayer is further rooted in the fascination with the mystery of the word, which has always characterized Jewish spirituality. Augmented by the Kabbalistic creation myth, in which God is said to create through the permutations of chains of Hebrew letters, it sets the mysticism of words and letters as one of the central themes of Jewish religious literature. [7]

Wisdom as the Divine Feminine

For both modern Jews and modern Christians, Proverbs' personification of Wisdom is significant in the way it associates God with feminine characteristics. When Wisdom begins to speak in Proverbs 8, she speaks as a woman. That is no small matter; the feminine aspects of Wisdom shape her character. Within Proverbs, this imagining evolves in three stages. At first, Wisdom is a simple abstraction, an allegorical figure dramatizing the role of God's wisdom in human life. As such, Wisdom's primary action is to call out to simple human beings to come to her for instruction:

> Wisdom cries out in the street;
>   in the squares she raises her voice.
> At the busiest corner she cries out;
>   at the entrance of the city gates she speaks:

7. *Your Word Is Fire*, ed. and trans. Arthur Green and Barry W. Holtz (New York: Paulist Press, 1977), 9.

"How long, O simple ones, will you love being simple?
. . . I will pour out my thoughts to you;
   I will make my words known to you." (Prov 1:20-23)

Wisdom's call is repeated at the beginning of chapter 8:

Does not wisdom call,
   and does not understanding raise her voice?
On the heights, beside the way,
   at the crossroads she takes her stand;
beside the gates in front of the town,
   at the entrance of the portals she cries out:
"To you, O people, I call . . .
O simple ones, learn prudence;
   acquire intelligence, you who lack it." (8:1-5)

Although this is simple allegory, there are three aspects of Wisdom's characterization that are surprising: first, unlike most instructors, she seeks out her students; second, she does not speak to them on some high and remote mountain but goes down into the streets of the city, even to "the busiest corner"; last but not least, she does not associate with those who are like-minded but with those who are unwise. In all these ways Wisdom exhibits her femininity because her focus is not on giving lofty instruction but on *making connections*. She goes to meet with her students wherever they are; she does not set herself apart but reaches out in empathy and tries to draw them to her.

When Wisdom's call is repeated for the third time at the beginning of chapter 9, her character increases in complexity. Wisdom is now imagined as a woman of substance with a house and servants, inviting people to her home for a feast:

Wisdom has built her house,
   she has hewn her seven pillars.
She has slaughtered her animals, she has mixed her wine,
   she has also set her table.

> She has sent out her servant-girls, she calls
> > from the highest places in town,
> "You that are simple, turn in here!"
> > To those without sense she says,
> "Come, eat of my bread
> > and drink of the wine I have mixed.
> Lay aside immaturity, and live,
> > and walk in the way of insight." (9:1-6)

Wisdom as a bountiful hostess deepens the image of her as a womanly figure, someone who is maternal and nurturing.

Wisdom further describes herself as God's constant companion; they experience mutual joy:

> and I was daily his delight,
> > rejoicing before him always,
> rejoicing in his inhabited world
> > and delighting in the human race. (8:30b-31)

As such, Wisdom expresses another feminine aspect of humanity: that part in all of us that "delights" in life, especially in loving and being loved. As we begin to picture Wisdom, she no longer seems an abstraction. Rather, she is the visible image of the joyful and creative love that brings forth and blesses human life.

At the very end of Proverbs, in a section set off as an acrostic poem, Wisdom reappears as the ideal wife. The poem opens with a question, "A capable wife who can find?" (31:10a). It is a question that subtly echoes Job: "Where shall wisdom be found?" (28:12). As the poet begins to describe what he is seeking, there are echoes of earlier descriptions of Wisdom. "She is far more precious than jewels" (31:10b), he says, reminding the reader of Wisdom's speech: "Take my instruction instead of silver . . . for Wisdom is better than jewels" (8:11). The poet also speaks of the honor and riches Wisdom's husband has achieved, reminding us further that Wisdom had said earlier, "Riches and honor are with me" (8:18). In the concluding verse of the poem, the speaker says: "[L]et her works praise her in the city gates" (31:31b), recalling that these gates have been the place of Wisdom (8:3).

The portrait of Wisdom here is filled out as never before. We are shown a woman who is faithful ("She does him [her husband] good and not harm, all the days of her life" [31:12]); industrious (she "works with willing hands" [31:13]); and, above all, provident, making sure that her husband and children and whole household have both food and clothing (31:15, 21). Her providence, like that of God, is practical ("with the fruit of her hands she plants a vineyard" [31:16b]), somewhat mysterious ("like the ships of the merchant, she brings her bread from far away" [31:14]), and in-clusively compassionate ("She opens her hand to the poor, and reaches out her hands to the needy" [31:20]). She speaks the lan-guage of Wisdom: "She opens her mouth with wisdom, and the teaching of kindness is on her tongue" (31:26). In conclusion, she is praised as one who has attained wisdom—as one who "fears the Lord" (31:30). When the author says her children and her husband praise her (31:28), he uses the word (*hallel*) for praising God.

As an aside, it seems worth noting here that this is a portrait of a strong woman. To call her "Lady Wisdom" is to evoke an elite social class that is not only anachronistic but trivializing. By the same token, to reject this portrait as too "domestic" (as some modern feminists have done) is to overlook its powerful and mys-tical elements. Here is a woman whose intelligent and compas-sionate care for others mirrors the very providence of God.

What we have in this portrait is neither an abstraction nor a personification of one of God's attributes but a portrayal of what Wisdom looks like in the flesh. The ideal woman shown here is Wisdom incarnate. The poet's model for this ideal woman may well have been his own wife. But the portrait he paints for us transcends ordinary human limitations. The poet has achieved a verbal *trompe l'oeil*. Looked at one way, here is a real woman who is wise; looked at another, she is Wisdom herself made flesh.

In the Song of Songs, Sirach, and the Wisdom of Solomon, the emphasis shifts from the characteristics of Wisdom to the relationship between Wisdom and those who seek her. In these works, this relationship is imagined as a love affair. In the Song, the love story has no ending; it is an experience of mutual and endless seeking and finding, then losing and seeking all over again. The rabbis called it a *mashal*—that is, a parable or riddle:

> Do not let this parable be light in your eyes, for by means of this parable one comes to comprehend the words of Torah. A parable to a king who has lost a gold coin from his home or a precious pearl—does he not find it by means of a wick worth a penny?[8]

What were they thinking? They imply that all of Torah represents a love story between God and human beings. The Song should not be dismissed as "only" erotic poetry. It is an eroticism that points to love as the creative energy and powerful attraction of God. Later, just as the rabbis saw the poem as the love song between God and Israel, so the church fathers interpreted it as the love song between Christ and the church. Both interpretations point to a sense of something deeper: to an ultimate love that is the renewing energy of the cosmos—"the love that moves the sun and the other stars."

Enlarging on the idea that "fear of the Lord" is wisdom, and that wisdom, in turn, is a source of human delight, Sirach speaks of Wisdom as both "a mother" and "a young bride" (15:2). She is the archetypal feminine, combining attractiveness with nurture:

> She will feed him with the bread of learning
>   and give him the water of wisdom to drink.
> He will lean on her and not fall,
>   and he will rely on her and not be put to shame. (Sir 15:3-4)

---

8. From the introduction to the Midrash on the Song of Songs.

Sirach also draws on images from the Song of Songs. It transfers to the seeker of wisdom the characteristics of the Song's lover. In the Song, the woman sees her lover coming and exclaims, "Look, there he stands behind our wall, gazing in at the windows, looking through the lattice" (Song 2:9). In a similar way Sirach says here, "Blessed is the person who meditates on wisdom . . . pursuing her like a hunter, and lying in wait on her paths; who peers through her windows and listens at her doors; who camps near her house . . . who pitches his tent near her" (14:20-25). Following the imagery of the whole work, we find an exchange between the lovers—the wisdom-seeker "pitches his tent" near Wisdom; Wisdom pitches her tent near the beloved.

Wisdom also speaks of herself in ways that echo the beloved woman of the Song. There, the lover describes the woman as "stately as a palm tree" (7:7), and the woman invites him to "Come" and enjoy her beauty (7:11). In Sirach, Wisdom says of herself, "I grew tall like a palm tree in En-gedi" (24:14), and she says to her lover, "Come to me, you who desire me, and eat your fill of my fruits" (24:19).

In effect, what Sirach has done is to dramatize the rabbinic interpretation of the Song as a parable relating to the Torah. As Wisdom is identified with the Torah, the one who meditates on the Torah is imagined as a lover. At the end of his work, the author appends an acrostic poem about his love for Wisdom—how he sought her and delighted in her. He urges others to follow his example:

> Put your neck under her yoke
>   and let your souls receive instruction;
> it is to be found close by.
>
> See with your own eyes that I have labored but little
>   and found for myself much serenity. (Sir 51:26-27)

"Yoke" was a common word for the Torah; the author is suggesting that pursuing Wisdom through the Torah leads to a life of serenity.

Sirach was probably written before 180 BCE and translated into Greek circa 117. The Wisdom of Solomon is roughly contemporary, being dated around 169 BCE. Written in Greek by an anonymous Alexandrine Jew, the name "Solomon" is obviously a symbol. This Solomon pursues Wisdom with the same ardor as the seeker in Sirach:

> I loved her and sought her from my youth.
> I desired to take her for my bride,
> and became enamored of her beauty. (Wis 8:2)

The portrait of Wisdom herself, however, changes into a more ethereal, ontological being. Solomon's description of his beloved is not sensuous but spiritual:

> There is in her a spirit that is intelligent, holy,
> unique, manifold, subtle,
> mobile, clear, unpolluted,
> distinct, invulnerable, loving the good, keen,
> irresistible, beneficent, humane,
> steadfast, sure, free from anxiety,
> all-powerful, overseeing all,
> and penetrating through all spirits
> that are intelligent, pure, and altogether subtle.
> For wisdom is more mobile than any motion;
> because of her pureness she pervades and penetrates all
>   things. (7:22-24)

She shares in God's being, "a breath of the power of God, and a pure emanation of the glory of the Almighty" (7:25). She is God's image: "a reflection of eternal light, a spotless mirror of the working of God, and an image of his goodness" (7:26). She shares in God's cosmic power: "Although she is but one, she can do all things, and while remaining in herself, she renews all things" (7:27a). She is a spirit that enters human beings and transforms them: "in every generation she passes into holy souls and makes them friends of God, and prophets" (7:27b).

In Proverbs, Wisdom evolves into God's cocreator and then is imagined as an ideal woman. In the Song she is the beloved, ceaselessly sought and loved. In Sirach she inheres in God's gift of the Torah. And in the Wisdom of Solomon, she is both God's image and God's holy spirit, capable of entering into human beings and changing them so that they too are a reflection of the divine.

From the Personification of Wisdom to the Person of Christ

What did it mean, then, for the early Jewish followers of Christ to speak of Christ as the Word or Wisdom of God? Surely the Jewish understanding of the mysticism of God's word was in the mind of John when he began his gospel:

> In the beginning was the Word,
> and the Word was with God,
> and the Word was God.

Even before John, the tradition of Wisdom as the beginning of Creation must have been in the mind of the author of the Letter to the Colossians when he described Christ as "the firstborn of all creation, for in him all things in heaven and earth were created, things visible and invisible. . . . He himself is before all things. . . . He is the beginning" (Col 1:15-18).

Literary allusions are a shortcut to meaning. When the Pauline author of Colossians and John the Evangelist wanted to interpret to their communities what Christ meant to them, they reminded their respective audiences of the ancient portrait of Wisdom in Proverbs 8. They were not offering the definitions of systematic theology that have come to dominate Western thought. Rather, they were offering a mystical image that modern Christians need to ponder for its poetic implications. As later readers of Colossians and John's gospel, we need to meditate on this image in order to grasp what is being said.

Wisdom says she was beside God as God's *amon* (Prov 8:30). The word can mean *architect* or *artisan, confidant,* or *foster child.* However one translates it, the word suggests that Wisdom has an intimacy with God that is different from everything else. Even if created, Wisdom is not a creature in the sense of the mountains and the sea. Whether artisan, confidant, or child, the word indicates that Wisdom has a consciousness and creativity akin to God's own. Her chief characteristic is joy:

> I was daily [God's] delight,
> rejoicing before God always,
> rejoicing in [God's] inhabited world
> and delighting in the human race. (Prov 8:30-31)

The figure created by the author of Proverbs is multilayered and rich in possibilities. As cocreator, or confidant, or child of God, she is imagined as a joyful, mediating figure between divinity and humanity. It is this aspect of her being that seized the imagination of Athanasius, chief architect of the fourth-century Nicene Creed. In one of his treatises against downplaying the divinity of Jesus, Athanasius focuses on the mutual delight between Wisdom and God. Using the Gospel of John as the primary basis for his theological argument, Athanasius interprets it through the lens of Proverbs' Wisdom:

> and the Father rejoices in the Son, and in this same joy the Son delights in the Father, saying, "I was beside him, his delight. Day by day, I rejoiced in his presence" (Prov. 8:30). When was it that the Father did not rejoice? But if he has always rejoiced, then there was always one in whom he rejoiced. (*Against the Arians* 82.2)

In other words, Athanasius interprets the Gospel of John as identifying Jesus with Wisdom—*as Wisdom describes herself in Proverbs 8.* So we, readers of another time, must ask ourselves: Did John

think of Proverbs 8 when he wrote about "the Word" in his Prologue? The idea seems startling to our age because it seems to
violate our assumptions about the writing of Scripture, which are
disposed towards the historical. But perhaps we need to consider
Athanasius's assumptions. He apparently found it natural to assume
that John would have described Christ through the lens of an
ancient biblical text. His assumptions coincide with what Fishbane
says were the working practices of ancient Israel. What Fishbane
describes seems to fit what John does. So we must ask ourselves:
Would the gospel writers have been inclined to follow the sacred
practice of reinterpreting Scripture that Fishbane describes? Three
of them were religious Jews and the fourth (Luke) was known as
a "God-fearer"—that is, someone attracted to the beliefs and ways
of Judaism. The kind of theologizing that Fishbane describes was
their theological context. Would they not have followed the theological practice of their time and used Scripture as a way to interpret their religious insights? We know that Jesus of Nazareth was
someone whose very life and death and resurrection opened up for
them new scriptural meanings. It would not have been appropriate
for them to write a biography like the Greeks and the Romans,
who emphasized the importance of human achievement; it was
Jewish to want to show the importance of *God*'s achievement. They
wanted to show how Jesus of Nazareth "opened the Scriptures to
them" (Luke 24:32)—not only by what he said (which, for the most
part, was not unique) but by the way he lived and died and rose
again. When they asked themselves the typical rabbinic question,
"What was he *like*?" they would have heard the scriptural response:
He is like God's Word, God's Wisdom, living among us.

In the next chapters I will discuss the large ways in which the
evangelists drew on the traditions of Wisdom in their presentation
of Christ. But a few points might be mentioned here. First of all,
Christ, like Wisdom, seeks out his disciples; he does not remain
remote from them but goes to busy places to find them. Second,
he does not seek out those who are already wise but rather those
who are foolish—not the righteous, but sinners. Third, Wisdom's

speech in Sirach, inviting those who are overburdened to submit to her yoke instead (51:26-27), is echoed by Jesus in Matthew: "Come to me, all you who labor and are burdened. . . . Take my yoke upon you and learn from me, for I am meek and humble of heart, and you will find rest" (Matt 11:28-30).

And beyond these small, immediate comparisons, it is helpful to reflect on the large characterization of Christ in the gospels, where he is portrayed as fully masculine in strength but also fully feminine in his sensibilities. He worries about those who are hungry, whether a little girl (Mark 5:43) or a large crowd (Mark 6:39-44; 8:1-8; Matt 15:32; John 6:5); he weeps, both over the fate of a large city (Matt 23:37; Luke 19:41-42) and over the loss of a friend (John 11:35). He does not try to seize power but models lowly service (John 13:12-14). (I am drawing on stereotypes here, assuming that human wholeness involves both masculine and feminine traits—both *yin* and *yang*—and that we all have some of each.)

In the Gospel of Mark, one is struck by the hiddenness of Christ's identity, what many scholars have dubbed "the messianic secret."[9] In conventional stereotypes, masculine speech is expected to be forthright and obvious, while feminine speech is expected to be less revealing, disclosing the self more gradually. The mystery of the woman is part of her allure; unknown, she attracts followers. Within this stereotypical pattern, masculine speech is straightforward, blunt, rational, and clear; feminine speech is indirect, emotional, intuitive, and imaginative. Parables and proverbs are "feminine" speech. The desire to be in control, to "lord it over" others, is a masculine trait; the contrasting desire to be of service is a feminine one. Above all, the willingness to lose one's life in order to give birth to new life belongs to the feminine side of our nature.

The teachings of Christ in the Gospel of Matthew are remarkably feminine in content. At least five of the eight Beatitudes that

9. See William Wrede, *The Messianic Secret*, trans. J. C. Grieg (Greenwood, SC: Attic Press, 1971).

form the substance of the Sermon on the Mount (Matt 5) extol feminine virtues: the willingness to acknowledge one's dependence on God and thus be "poor in spirit"; the disposition to comfort those who mourn; the honesty about oneself that constitutes meekness; the instinct to be merciful (to carry another "in the womb"); the desire to make peace. The parables that Christ tells in Matthew emphasize the feminine way of seeing human beings as never fully finished but always in process: the weeds allowed to grow among the wheat; the treasure discovered in the field that has yet to be possessed; the pearl of great price that has to be searched for; the wide net thrown into the sea that will bring up all manner of things that can be sorted out later. Matthew's emphasis on forgiving over judging (Matt 18) is a deeply feminine virtue. Above all, Matthew's vision of the Last Judgment is remarkable for its lack of absolute judgments of any kind: people are judged not in terms of laws but in terms of relationships.

The Gospel of Luke emphasizes God's Spirit as the divine energy that, like Solomon's "Wisdom," is a feminine force that "enters into holy souls and makes them friends of God" (Wis 7:27). The feminine nature of this energy is expressed by Luke through his opening scenes: first, Mary and Elizabeth meet as two pregnant women, large with new life; Mary and Zechariah respond to the births of their sons; Simeon and Anna greet the holy child in the temple. It is also expressed stylistically through a series of songs: Mary's *Magnificat* and Zechariah's canticle about his son; the "Glory to God" of the shepherds; Simeon's *Nunc dimittis*. Luke also adds episodes to the gospel story that feature women: the raising up of the widow's son (7:11); the vignette of Martha and Mary (10:38); the healing of the crippled woman in the temple (13). He also adds teachings in which feminine values are dominant: the parable of the Good Samaritan, in which mercy trumps the rules; the parables of the Lost Sheep, the Lost Coin, and the Prodigal Son, in which God is imagined ceaselessly seeking (like a mother) to bring her children home. When Christ teaches about prayer in Luke, he stresses the feminine nagging of the Importunate Widow and the meekness of the Publican.

In John's gospel, as we have seen, he opens with language that echoes the description of feminine Wisdom in Proverbs 8. Although he uses the masculine noun *logos* instead of the feminine *sophia*, John describes Christ as "the Word" that has the life-giving quality of Proverbs' Wisdom ("All things came into being through him" [1:3]) and the same kind of love relationship to God ("close to the Father's heart," or "bosom" [1:18]). Unlike any other gospel, John the Baptist witnesses to Christ here as "the lamb of God"—a word that connotes either a sacrifice or a servant, both stereotypically connected to the feminine side of humanity. Christ's first miracle in John is to enhance the celebration of a wedding—an event always of feminine importance because its function is to unite human beings and to start new life. Throughout this gospel, Christ speaks in metaphorical language, which his literal-minded audience fails to grasp. In particular, he describes himself in a series of symbols: I am . . . the living water, the bread of life, the light of the world, the good shepherd, the gate, the vine. At a peak moment in the narrative, Christ acts out the role of a servant and washes the feet of his disciples (13). He then proclaims a new commandment: "Love one another as I have loved you" (13:34-35; 15:12). His love is not portrayed as an abstract concept but as a deep feeling (he weeps over Lazarus; 11:35) as well as a humble act of service (the washing of the feet). He exhibits a feminine concern for where people dwell: "I go to prepare a place for you" (14:2); "I will not leave you orphaned" (14:18). Eleven times he uses the word "abide" (15:4-10). He explains the disciples' future transformation in terms of a woman who experiences pain in labor but who forgets her sorrow "for joy that her child has been born" (16:21). His farewell prayer for his followers is for their unity. And his final meeting with his closest disciples stresses a personal relationship of love ("Peter, do you love me?" [21:15-17]).

Remarkably, the imagery of Proverbs 8 did not end with the gospels. It has also reached into modern times through the poetic thought of the East—that of Russian Orthodox theologians and, subsequently, of Thomas Merton. "Holy Wisdom" (*Hagia Sophia*) is central to Merton's contemplative vision, appearing not only in the poem by that name but also in his sketches of a young Jewish woman, whom he called "Proverb." Christopher Pramuk, writing about Merton's fascination with this figure, relates it directly to the woman in Proverbs 8:22:

> And in this "general dance" between God and the world, the human person mysteriously holds a special place as image and icon of God. Here the Wisdom literature of the Bible boldly, almost recklessly, celebrates the connecting threads—the liminal spaces!—between God and the cosmos and the human race "from before the beginning." And here Merton and the Russian Orthodox theologians of Wisdom . . . took their cues especially from Proverbs 8, where Sophia, the feminine Wisdom Child, emerges as a kind of go-between in creation.[10]

Pramuk goes on to quote the whole portrait of Wisdom in Proverbs 8:22-31, suggesting that the figure of Wisdom here evokes "not only the presence of Christ, the uncreated Wisdom of God who orders and 'plays' in the universe but also, through Christ's humanity, as it were, the primordial presence of the human race, created Sophia, in whom God rejoices and delights always."[11]

It is surprising to see how close this vision is to that of Athanasius. The text of Proverbs 8 suggested to Athanasius that Christ is preexistent, one with the Father, a cocreator, and "begotten, not made." He was not making metaphysical connections but imaginative ones. The language of Proverbs 8 was clearly in Athanasius's mind when he formed the phrases of the Nicene Creed:

---

10. *At Play in Creation* (Collegeville, MN: Liturgical Press, 2015), 22. Also see *Sophia: The Hidden Christ of Thomas Merton* (Collegeville, MN: Liturgical Press, 2009).

11. *At Play in Creation*, 23–24.

I believe in one Lord Jesus Christ,
the only-begotten son of God,
born of the Father before all ages . . .
begotten not made,
consubstantial with the Father,
through him all things were made.

By interpreting these phrases as statements of objective fact, we have lost the poetry of their origin. We seem to have forgotten that poetry has its own truth.

The poetry of Athanasius's vision can be heard in his prayer still offered by every priest before the moment of eucharistic consecration:

By the mystery of this water and wine
may we come to share in the divinity of Christ
who humbled himself to share in our humanity.

How can ordinary human beings share in the divinity of Christ? It is a prayer that boldly implies the kind of transformation of being that is part of Teilhard's mystical vision.

The Transforming Effect of the Divine Feminine

To understand that vision fully, it is important to grasp Teilhard's comprehension of the divine Feminine at work in all of us. It is noteworthy that early on in his writings, Teilhard chose to transpose Proverbs 8 into the language of science.[12] In the quote given at the head of the chapter, he indicates his belief that the Feminine is an indispensable part of human nature—as necessary as "light, oxygen, or vitamins." Although he does not talk explicitly about the way the Feminine pervades the gospels, he implies

12. See "The Feminine or the Unitive," in *Heart of Matter*, 59. Also see "The Eternal Feminine," in *Writings in Time of War*, trans. René Hague (New York: Harper and Row, 1968), 191–202.

its significance in the person of Christ, describing him as "the great attracter." Elsewhere, he speaks of the Feminine as the "unitive" element in human beings. And he sees it as necessary not only within each person but also between them, attracting and binding persons to one another as part of the vast harmony of divine, creative love. He calls it "the Break-through into Amorization." He says:

> "Even after the flash of illumination in which the individual is suddenly revealed to himself, elementary Man would remain but half complete if he did not come into contact with the other sex and so, under the centric attraction of person-to-person, explode into flame."[13]

13. *Heart of Matter*, 60.

4

Mark
God's Wisdom Hidden in the Riddle of the Christ

> "As a direct consequence of the unitive process by which God is revealed to us, he in some way 'transforms' himself as he incorporates us. So . . . we have . . . to disclose Him . . . ever more fully."[1]

A parable in common understanding is a simple story that illustrates a moral or religious point. Such a definition derives logically from the Greek word for parable (*parabole*), which means "to lay alongside" or to illustrate. In Hebrew, however, the word for parable (*mashal*) has the added connotation of "riddle"—something puzzling and hidden. In Jewish hermeneutic tradition, moreover, a parable was often constructed out of scriptural allusions and served to interpret Scripture.

In chapter 4 of the Gospel of Mark, Jesus' disciples ask him about parables, and he responds:

1. Teilhard de Chardin, *The Heart of Matter*, 53.

To you has been given the secret of the kingdom of God, but
for those outside, everything comes in parables; in order that
"they may indeed look, but not perceive,
and may indeed listen, but not understand;
so that they may not turn again and be forgiven." (4:11-12)

Jesus' reply raises more questions than it answers. What is "the secret" (or mystery) of the kingdom of God, and how has it been given to the disciples? How is Jesus' way of communicating to his disciples different from the way he communicates with everyone else? And what does he mean by the final section in quotes—does he really speak in parables so that his listeners will not grasp his meaning and so will not be saved?

The quoted words are those of God sending Isaiah off on his prophetic mission (Isa 6:6-8). In that context they are obviously ironic: of course God wants the people to hear the prophet. So we too should understand the words as ironic here. The irony cloaks meaning in mystery so that we must reflect to unravel it. We cannot dismiss the passage too quickly because we need to slow down and engage with the seeming absurdity of the text. And in the process of that engagement we may arrive at a deeper level of meaning.

As we ponder the meaning here, it is also worth noting that before this chapter in Mark, Jesus has not told any parables. In fact, he has said very little. For the most part, he has just acted, and his actions have had a similar, puzzling effect. He has acted in ways that surprise and challenge conventional expectations. He does not condemn or avoid a man possessed by an unclean spirit but sets about releasing him (1:23-27). He eats with sinners and defends the potential spirituality of feasting (2:15-19). Instead of keeping up the conventional hedge around religious rules (the conventional "hedge around the Torah") he breaks through, exposing their essential purpose (2:23-27). He heals everyone who asks for it, regardless, it seems, of circumstance—as, for example, in the healing of the leper (3:1-5). He redefines the boundaries of "family," including all who do the will of the Father (3:31-35). And he teaches that all sins will be forgiven except blasphemy against the Holy Spirit (3:28-30). It is a teaching that has caused much controversy, with many arguing that he has a singular and mysterious sin in mind. But in context, he seems to be pitting the *Holy* Spirit against an *unclean* spirit: Jesus' exorcisms have shown that he regards possession by an unclean spirit to be a pathology, while possession by God's Holy Spirit is the intended human destiny.

His actions as well as his teachings confront us with the image of a person who consistently does and says the unexpected. We, the readers, like those inside the narrative, do not find his meaning obvious; we need to reflect on what he is about. In effect, before we hear Jesus tell a single parable, he functions as a riddling parable himself—that is, a story whose meaning is hidden, a story that requires unpacking.

A few verses after his first comment on the purpose of parables, Jesus offers a second comment: "Is a lamp brought in to be placed under the bushel basket, or under the bed, and not on the lampstand? For there is nothing hidden except to be disclosed; nor is anything secret except to come to light" (4:21-22). This second statement of purpose confirms the ironic reading of the first because it makes clear that Jesus' intention is to shed light, not to obfuscate. Jesus suggests that the parable itself is meant to be an explanation—a "lamp" shedding light on God's word. At the same time, his words indicate that God's word is "hidden" and needs light. What should we make of this?

Fishbane argues that Jews recognized the limits of human beings to grasp all of God's revelation all at once and so reckoned that each successive faith community would discover new aspects of God's revelation surfacing, as it were, in new contexts. The result was a constant rewriting of biblical texts in order to show their relevance to the contemporary time. This rewriting was interpretive yet, unlike modern interpretations, did not involve direct analysis or exposition. Instead, these interpreters wove new narratives out of the old ones. The new narrative was intended to shed light on God's word, yet its meaning was not transparent. Woven out of pieces of Scripture, it contained allusions that were "hidden." These allusions engage the reader in a process of discovery.

Jesus' parables in Mark are like that. Woven out of scriptural quotes or allusions, they comprise what Fishbane termed "inner-biblical exegesis." Readers must know the original biblical words in order to grasp the significance of later narratives that build on them. If readers are unaware of the first biblical text, then later meanings will be lost on them; they will "look but not perceive, listen but not understand."

If we apply this understanding to Jesus' statements about parables, we will find his meaning clearer. When, for example, Jesus tells the parable of the Sower, he is making use of a common biblical comparison between God's word and the processes of nature. As Isaiah describes it, God says:

> For as the rain and snow come down from heaven,
>   and do not return there until they have watered the earth,
> making it bring forth and sprout,
>   giving seed to the sower and bread to the eater,
> so shall my word be that goes out from my mouth;
>   it shall not return to me empty,
> but it shall accomplish that which I purpose,
>   and succeed in the thing for which I sent it. (Isa 55:10-11)

When the disciples question him about the Sower, Jesus expresses his surprise in different ways. First, as we have seen, he tells them, "[T]he mystery of the kingdom of God has been granted to you." Implicitly, they have direct access to the mystery in the person of Jesus. "But," Jesus continues, "for those outside, everything comes in parables." "Those outside," it now appears, are those outside God's word. If one does not know God's word to begin with, one has no way of grasping its relevance.

Next, we hear Jesus expressing surprise at the disciples' ignorance of this particular parable: "Do you not understand this parable? Then how will you understand all the parables?" (4:13). He is saying that the comparison of God's word to a seed is basic to all understanding of Scripture; like a seed, God's word is intended to grow and germinate and multiply in human understanding.

Finally, Jesus indicates, as we have seen, that a parable is like a lamp meant to illuminate the meaning of God's word. This view is congenial with the rabbinic one that introduces the Midrash on the Song of Songs:

> Do not let this parable be light in your eyes, for by means of this parable one comes to comprehend the words of Torah. A parable to a king who has lost a gold coin from his home or a precious pearl—does he not find it by means of a wick worth a penny?

The rabbis are suggesting that a parable aids the reader in the same way as a small, penny-wick candle helps a king find precious things he has not been able to see. The parable is intended to illuminate the scriptural word that is hidden within it.

The three seed parables of Mark 4 are good examples. In the first parable, the hyperbolic contrast between the fate of the seed sown in different kinds of soil echoes the apocalyptic perspective of the time. Just as in the book of Daniel some awaken after death to "shame and contempt" and others to "everlasting life" (Dan 12:2), so in Jesus' parable some seeds are devoured, scorched, and choked, while others bring forth grain "yielding thirty and sixty and a hundredfold" (Mark 4:8).

In the second seed parable, the relaxed attitude of the sower towards the seed is comically nonapocalyptic. Significantly, the wise person is described in a way that echoes the ultimate wisdom of the Preacher of Ecclesiastes:

> Whoever observes the wind will not sow;
>   and whoever regards the clouds will not reap.
> Just as you do not know how the breath comes to the bones
> in the mother's womb, so you do not know the work of God,
> who makes everything. (Eccl 11:4-5)

So the sower here "does not know how" the seed sprouts and grows (Mark 4:27). The echo turns the sower's detachment from the seed into benign neglect, one prompted not by indifference but by trust.

The parable of the mustard seed takes its full meaning from the way it echoes Ezekiel. While everyone hears the contrast between "the smallest of all the seeds" and "the greatest of all shrubs," a Jewish audience of the first century would have heard something more—namely, the "noble cedar" that God plants in Ezekiel, one so great that "birds can nest in its shade" (Ezek 17:22-23; Mark 4:32). It is a tree that both in Ezekiel and in Daniel (4:7b-9)—and here again in Mark—symbolizes the kingdom of God.

These analogues are not simple comparisons. God's kingdom is not being compared to a seed as a static object. Rather, the kingdom is being related to a sequence of actions, a whole process: "Listen! A sower went out to sow. And as he sowed" (Mark 4:3-4); "The kingdom of heaven is as if someone would scatter seed" (Mark 4:26); "It is like a mustard seed, which, when sown upon the ground" (Mark 4:31). To understand the analogue, we need to follow the entire dynamic. What is more, each analogue is echoing concepts, images, and phrases of Scripture (Daniel, Ecclesiastes, Ezekiel) that give it a further layer of meaning.

The fullest meaning is revealed by the linking of these three, quite different, analogues. Joined together, they are reminders that the scriptural tradition offers more than one way to regard God's reign: as a final judgment in which only a few become fit for harvest; as an inevitable outcome of God's benevolence in which we must trust but can take no credit; as a highly accessible, common experience of growth into glory. Taken together, the three parables look at the meaning of God's kingdom from three different angles, evoking our deepest fears and our deepest hopes.

This juxtaposition of different scriptural views is typical of midrashic commentary, which often jars the biblical reader awake by exposing contradictory voices within the tradition. Awareness of the contradiction raises questions for the readers, who must then grapple with how to interpret the tradition for their own time. So here, within this chapter in Mark, Jesus does not resolve the distance between the parables or choose among its perspectives. He leaves his listeners to ponder the tension in the tradition and the puzzle inherent in its contrasting images.[2]

This challenge of contrasting scriptural perspectives tends to make a parable more of a riddle than simply an illustrative story—that is, something that teases or confounds the mind. To borrow from another Near Eastern tradition, it is not unlike the Buddhist *koan*, a riddle that awakens the mind by confronting it with the nonrational. (For example: "What is the sound of one hand clapping?")

The Midrash often offers this kind of narrative, one that both confounds and stimulates. Jacob Neusner has noted that the biblical verse most often pondered by rabbis in the first century was Genesis 1:26, which describes human beings as made in God's image.[3] Here is one example of the Midrash on this verse, which highlights the paradox it contains:

> When the Holy One, blessed be He, created a human being,
> the ministering angels mistook him [for a divine being] and
> wished to exclaim "Holy" before him. (*Genesis Rabbah* 8.10)

And here is another Midrash on the same theme, one that keeps Genesis 1:26 in mind even while reflecting on the place in Leviticus where God says, "I will be ever in your midst." "The meaning of this," says the Midrash, "is to be expressed by means of parable":

---

2. For the function of this kind of tension, see Daniel Boyarin, *Intertextuality and the Reading of Midrash* (Bloomington: Indiana University Press, 1990), 77–78. The labored allegorical explanation of the first parable (Mark 4:14-20) was probably not Mark's but the addition of some later editor. See Vincent Taylor, *The Gospel According to Saint Mark* (London: Macmillan, 1963), 258.

3. See Bruce Chilton and Jacob Neusner, *Judaism in the New Testament* (New York: Routledge, 1995), 175–78.

> To what may this be likened? To a king who went out to
> stroll in his orchard with his tenant farmer and the tenant
> kept hiding himself from the presence of the king. So the
> king said to that tenant, "Why do you hide from me? Be-
> hold, I, you—we're alike." Similarly in the Age to Come the
> Holy One, blessed be He, will stroll with the righteous in
> the Garden of Eden, but when the righteous see Him they
> will tremble before him; and the Holy One, blessed be He,
> will say to him, "Why is it that you tremble before me?
> Behold, I, you—we're alike." (*Sifre* on Lev 26:12)

In each case, the midrashic narrative draws on our conventional
ideas of the distance between God and humanity and overturns
them. Both confront the mind with something that is seemingly
unreasonable: angels worshiping a human being; God strolling
with a human being. The confounding aspect of these stories turns
them into riddles, teasing the mind. They illumine their respective
texts not by explaining them but by retelling their meaning in a
different way.

Jesus also confronts his listeners with a direct riddle when he
asks them,

> How can the scribes say that the Messiah is the son of
> David? David himself, by the Holy Spirit, declared,
>   "The Lord said to my Lord,
>   'Sit at my right hand,
>   until I put your enemies under your feet.'"
> David himself calls him Lord; so how can he be his son?
> (Mark 12:35-36)

Here again the riddling aspect of Jesus' question can only be
understood if one knows the scriptural traditions underlying it.
First of all, Jesus draws here on the common first-century understanding that David was the author of all the psalms. He then
achieves a challenging tension by melding the first verse from
Psalm 110 with the sixth verse from Psalm 8. In Psalm 110 God

says to his anointed, "Sit at my right hand until I make your enemies your footstool." In Psalm 8 the psalmist muses in wonder about all God has given to human beings: "You have put all things under [their] feet." In blending these two verses, Jesus creates a surprising equation between "the anointed" of Psalm 110 and the ordinary human being, who is the subject of Psalm 8. The juxtaposition raises the question of what is meant by God's "anointed"— that is, God's *messiah*. Is Jesus implying that every person is, in some sense, God's anointed?

Scripture, dealing with mystery, is designed to raise questions, not give answers. And just as Jesus makes no overt choice between the seed analogues for God's kingdom, so here he does not answer his own question. Mark shows him simply shaking up the conventional idea of a messiah as an invulnerable victor (the notion that Peter mistakenly had [8:31-33]), so that Jesus' own identity can redefine it. Note that Mark shows Jesus constantly referring to himself not as the "messiah" but as the "son of man"—the key phrase that describes all human beings in Psalm 8.

By juxtaposing contrasting views of Scripture, these parables raise questions, and these questions, in turn, open up hitherto hidden possibilities of meaning. For example, we might be tempted to take the first seed parable of apocalyptic doom as expressing Jesus' own perspective, were it not juxtaposed to two decidedly different views of God's kingdom. Over the centuries most have read the parables in isolation, not being sensitized to Jewish practices of indirect interpretation. Yet once one is made aware of this subtle habit of undermining one point of view by juxtaposing another, one sees that the second and third parables reverse the meaning of the first. In the same way, the meaning of Jesus' question about the messiah can only be fully grasped if one is aware of the way it has juxtaposed two psalms, each with a different view of God's relationship with humanity. Once one sees this juxtaposition, one is forced to ponder: if God has made each of us "a little lower than God" (Ps 8:5), has God made each of us part of God's self? In short, in each case it is the riddle itself that holds the revelation.

Across all four gospels the evangelists show Jesus telling sixty parables; they comprise more than a third of what he says. One cannot escape the implication that the evangelists saw him as a rabbi and a midrashist, an interpreter of Scripture. What is more, they composed in this tradition themselves, using its rhetorical strategies of biblical interweavings and riddling paradox to indicate that they saw him as a living parable in himself.[4]

At the end of chapter 4, Mark describes an episode in which Jesus "rebukes" the sea and the wind, and his disciples, "filled with awe," say to one another, "Who then is this, that even the wind and the sea obey him?" (Mark 4:41). Like the parables that Jesus has just told, this episode is composed of a sequence of actions that echo phrases or moments of Scripture. The sequence begins with the disciples in a boat with Jesus and the sudden coming up of "a great windstorm"—one so violent, in fact, that "waves beat into the boat" (Mark 4:37). There is an echo here of Psalm 69, where the psalmist calls out to God, "Save me, O God, for the waters have come up to my neck. . . . I have come into deep waters, and the flood sweeps over me" (Ps 69:1, 2b). It also recalls the narrative of Psalm 107:

> Some went down to the sea in ships . . .
>> their courage melted away in their calamity; . . .
> Then they cried to the Lord in their trouble,
>> and he brought them out from their distress;
> he made the storm be still,
>> and the waves of the sea were hushed. (vv. 23-29)

---

4. Others have had this basic insight but in substantially different ways. See John Donahue, who says that "Jesus himself is parable; so also the Gospel presentations of him." *The Gospel in Parable* (Philadelphia: Fortress Press, 1988), 9. Also see Stephen Moore, *Mark and Method: New Approaches in Biblical Studies* (Minneapolis: Fortress Press, 1992), 87–88. Most recently, J. D. Crossan has offered that view of Jesus; see *The Power of Parable* (San Francisco: Harper One, 2012).

Similarly distressed, the disciples look for Jesus' help but find he is "asleep on the cushion" in the stern of the boat (Mark 4:38). The whole scene echoes the moment in the book of Jonah when the sailors, alarmed by the storm that is tossing their boat, look for Jonah and find him sleeping (Jonah 1:4-5). It also brings to mind the parable of the farmer asleep while his seed keeps growing. The parallels are not exact in either case, but they are evocative. Jonah had to be thrown overboard before the storm would subside; he becomes the scapegoat that saves the boat. The sleeping farmer only appears to be negligent; implicit is his trust that God will bring the seed to harvest.

The disciples waken Jesus with a question that recalls many psalms: "Do you not care that we are perishing?" (Mark 4:38). The conclusion of the episode is filled with reminders of many psalms that are riffs on God's separation of earth from sea in Genesis 1:

> He woke up, rebuked the wind, and said to the sea, "Peace! Be still!" Then the wind ceased, and there was a dead calm. . . . And they [the disciples] were filled with great awe and said to one another, "Who then is this, that even the wind and the sea obey him?" (Mark 4:39-41)

In Genesis, God creates land by separating the earth from the sea; God gathers the waters together and so makes space for dry land. This is similar to God's action in parting the sea so that the Israelites could escape from slavery; each time, God creates by rearranging what is there. God's power to reorder and so create, to tame the sea and open up new space, is deeply embedded in the Jewish psyche. It is celebrated in the psalms:

> O LORD God of hosts,
>> who is as mighty as you? . . .
> You rule the raging of the sea;
>> when its waves rise, you still them. (Ps 89:8a, 9)

You silence the roaring of the seas,
the roaring of their waves. (Ps 65:7)

He made the storm be still;
and the waves of the sea were hushed. (Ps 107:29)

These psalms are echoed here in the question of the disciples: "Who then is this, that even the wind and the sea obey him?" The question suggests that Jesus' action reflects that of God in the act of creation. So Mark shows Jesus himself to be a parable, an analogue of what God is like.

Understanding Jesus as himself a parable or riddle throws light on everything else in Mark's gospel. The opening word of Mark is "beginning," a word that the rabbis taught was a synonym for "wisdom." Accordingly, they interpreted the opening verse of the Bible to mean, "In *Wisdom*, God created the heavens and the earth."[5] Thus by starting with *beginning* (with no article before it), Mark opens his gospel by reminding his readers of the opening of Genesis and of how God creates through his Word, his Wisdom. Understood in this context, Mark's first words may be understood to mean, "The *wisdom* of the gospel of Jesus Christ," a phrase that can mean both Jesus' teachings and *who Jesus is*, his very identity.

The scene of Jesus' baptism confirms and deepens this theme: "And just as he was coming up out of the water, he saw the heavens torn apart and the Spirit descending like a dove on him. And a voice came from heaven, 'You are my Son, the Beloved; with you I am well pleased'" (Mark 1:10-11).

Elisha, in succeeding Elijah, receives a double portion of his spirit (2 Kgs 1:9-12); Jesus, in succeeding John, receives God's own Spirit. In biblical tradition, God's Holy Spirit is yet another synonym for God's Wisdom, so Mark's choice of vocabulary repeats and emphasizes that Jesus is identified with God's Wisdom. "I have baptized

5. James Kugel, *The Bible as It Was* (Cambridge, MA: Harvard University Press, 1997), 53–57.

you with water," John says, "but he will baptize you with the Holy Spirit" (Mark 1:8). Jesus, receiver of God's Wisdom, will immerse his followers in it. The water out of which Jesus rises is like the waters of the first creation that God's Word shaped into life. The "beloved son" echoes Genesis 22:2, the phrase describing Isaac, Abraham's promised son who is to bear God's blessing to all people. At the same time, the conjunction of "dove" and "beloved" echoes the Song of Songs, where each lover repeatedly calls the other "beloved,"[6] the woman is frequently compared to a dove (1:15; 2:14; 4:1; 6:9), and the season for love is signaled by "the voice of the turtledove . . . heard in our land" (2:12). As we have seen earlier, the rabbis perceived the Song to be a parable revealing God's love throughout the whole Bible; so here, the echoes of the Song at the beginning of Jesus' ministry are Mark's signal that another version of the divine-human love story is about to unfold.

A totally different aspect of the biblical tradition is implicated when Mark next tells us that "the Spirit straightway drove him out into the wilderness," where he stayed for forty days.[7] He was "tempted by Satan; and he was with the wild beasts; and the angels waited on him" (Mark 1:12-13). The echoes here are of Genesis 3:1-5, where Eve is tempted by the serpent, and of Genesis 3:24, where God drives the fallen human beings out of Eden; also of Exodus 23:20, where God promises to send an angel to lead the people to a new land. These echoes suggest that Jesus is not only an analogue for God but also an analogue for sin-prone human beings. He is a parable of vulnerable and divinized humanity all in one; he is the ultimate riddle.

6. Song 1:16; 2:8-10, 16-17; 4:16; 5:2, 4, 6, 8-10, 16; 6:1-3; 7:10-11, 13; 8:5, 14.

7. The NRSV translates "straightway" as "immediately," but the Greek word echoes the word for "straight" in v. 3: "Make straight the ways of the Lord." Mark is consciously putting together "straight" and "way," making a pun that works in both Greek and English. The King James preserves this pun by translating the word as "straightway."

As we have seen, the parable in Jewish tradition is often more than a narrative offering a simple comparison. It can be symbolic, scriptural, and interpretive all at once. And it may also be a riddle. So Mark presents Jesus to his readers as an iconic figure, woven out of Scripture. At the same time, Mark interprets Christ in a way that jolts and challenges the mind.

A riddle slows down the mind, forcing the listener to unpack its meaning. With similar effect, Mark delights in doublets, or in two versions of the same narrative. In chapter 8, Mark offers a clue to his craft. He narrates a second feeding miracle (Mark 8:1-9) and then offers another story that gives the key to his repetitiveness. The second story concerns the healing of a blind man in two stages. In the first stage of recovering his sight, the blind man can see only dim images but cannot distinguish one from another: "I can see people, but they look like trees, walking" (Mark 8:24). Then, after Jesus has "laid his hands on his eyes again, . . . he saw everything clearly" (Mark 8:25). If we reflect on the symbolic significance of this episode, we realize that Mark is telling us why so many key words and scenes in his gospel are repetitions or echoes, either of Old Testament passages or of scenes within the gospel itself, or of both. On one level we realize that Mark, as a skillful craftsman, provides us, his readers, with more than one scenario on the same theme so that we can move from dim comprehension to a clear grasp of his meaning. On another level, we realize that Mark is implying that his craft mirrors God's own; God repeats his miracles so that God's meaning may at last penetrate human blindness.

Looking at the gospel as a two-part structure, we can see that a turning point in both episode and speech occurs at the end of chapter 8 and the beginning of chapter 9. At the end of chapter 8, Jesus predicts his death for the first time (Mark 8:31), stresses that suffering will accompany those who follow him (Mark 8:34-35), and rebukes Peter for not understanding that "the [s]on of [m]an must undergo great suffering" (Mark 8:31). Up to this point in the gospel, there has been no talk of the need for anyone to suffer; on the contrary, Jesus has been engaged in the alleviation of suffering. In the first half of the gospel, miraculous healing is the norm; from this point onward, however, it is not. Jesus also stops speaking so constantly in parables and uses straightforward speech: he instructs his disciples plainly that exorcism is accomplished not through magic but through prayer (Mark 9:29), that the kingdom of heaven belongs to the childlike (Mark 10:14), that it is hard for "those who have wealth to enter the kingdom of God" (Mark 10:23), that "whoever wishes to be great among you must be your servant" (Mark 10:43), that forgiving others is the key to being forgiven (Mark 11:25), that the greatest commandment is to "love the Lord your God with all your heart, and with all your soul, with all your mind, and with all your strength" and "the second is this: 'You shall love your neighbor as yourself'" (Mark 12:30-31). All this is instruction in the process of self-emptying that reaches a climax in Jesus' death.

But there is another aspect to the turning point of the gospel: the scene of Jesus' transfiguration that opens chapter 9. While miracles and parables in the second part of the gospel nearly cease, this scene points to the ultimate miracle of human transformation. Jesus represents the riddle of human divinization. Mark's every word here signals something new is happening:

> Six days later, Jesus takes with him Peter and James and John, and leads them up a high mountain apart, by themselves. And he is transfigured before them, and his clothing becomes dazzling white, such as no one on earth could bleach them. (Mark 9:2-3 [my translation])

Although the verbs here are usually translated as past, the tense actually shifts to the historic present, suggesting a timeless moment. The "six days" remind us of the six days of creation and how God "blessed the seventh day and hallowed it" (Gen 2:3). It also reminds us of the six days Moses waited for God's voice on Mount Sinai and how "on the seventh day [God] called to Moses out of the cloud" (Exod 24:16b).

The word translated "transfigured" is actually "metamor-phosed"—that is, Mark does not say that Jesus changed just in appearance but that he changed in his very being. He next says that Jesus' clothing was gleaming white. As we have seen, that phrase was significant because it echoes a large number of Jewish writings of the time that imagined biblical figures ascending from earth to the heavens where they were newly clothed in radiant white garments. This Ascension literature expresses belief in the potential for human participation in the divine being; it expresses the idea that human beings are intended to become what Genesis calls them—the image of God. Here, in the very middle of his gospel (9:2-3), Mark shows Jesus in this transformed state—a human being reflecting the radiance of God.

The reaction of Peter is telling: "Rabbi, it is good for us to be here; let us make three dwellings [tabernacles], one for you, one for Moses, and one for Elijah" (Mark 9:5). The Greek word here for tabernacle (*skēnas*)—sometimes translated "booth" or "tent"—pointedly echoes the many places in the Old Testament where God is said to "tabernacle" with his people (Ezek 37:27; Joel 4:17; Zech 2:15; 8:3; Tob 13:10). It is also suggestive of the Jewish Feast of Tabernacles, an autumnal feast that celebrates the earthly harvest as a foretaste of the final one. All these echoes suggest that Peter recognizes the moment as a sacred time, requiring sacred space; he too, at least for this brief moment, has been transformed. The verse following confirms this: "He did not know what to say [because] they were filled with awe" (Mark 9:6).[8] The concluding phrase duplicates the one at 4:41; the disciples experience the same awe here as they did when Jesus stilled the sea. The implication is that in this moment, just as fully as in that earlier one, the disciples perceive the divinity within Jesus' humanity.

---

8. This last phrase has been conventionally translated "they were afraid," but the verb is exactly the same one used at the end of chapter 4 (*phobeomai*) to indicate the disciples' awe at Jesus' quieting of the storm.

Their perception is confirmed by the voice speaking out of the cloud, "This is my Son, the Beloved; listen to him" (Mark 9:7). The voice from the cloud echoes the voice speaking to Moses on Sinai; the words that the voice speaks echo the words of God at Jesus' baptism (Mark 1:11). The parallel between this scene and Sinai suggests a parallel between God's "Ten Words" to Moses and God's words about Jesus. In both cases, Mark is implying God is imparting God's wisdom to human beings. The parallel between this scene and Jesus' baptism makes this one of Mark's doublets. As such, the scene has a clarifying function, indicating that being God's Son means being transformed into God's image, reflecting God's radiance and wisdom.

When we come to the end of Mark's gospel we hear the words that identify Jesus as the son of God repeated again, this time by a Roman soldier after his death: "Truly this man was God's Son" (Mark 15:39). There are several things remarkable about this proclamation: first, that it is applied to someone hanging dead on a cross; second, that it is uttered by one of the very soldiers who was instrumental in his death; and third, that it stands in direct opposition to the idea of imperial power inscribed on the coin of the realm: "Caesar Augustus, Son of God." In all these ways, the scene confronts us with a paradox, a riddle. The pagan soldier's cry indicates that he has come to recognize God's transforming presence even in this most horrifying of human deaths.

Mark has also given us here a triad. The middle of the triad gives us the meaning that illuminates the other two parts: the human being as "son of God" is the human being as God's image. In Mark's portrayal of Jesus, this image is writ large and illumined at the moment of his transfiguration; it is also what is there, if we have the eyes to see it, in his death. The three linked episodes are progressively illuminating for the reader. When the heavenly voice calls Jesus "my beloved son" in the first instance, we, the readers, cannot be sure of its meaning; in the second instance, we, along with the disciples, are awed by the implications of divinity; in the third and last, we are brought to understand that God's life in us does not keep us from death but transforms it. Jesus' giving of himself in death is shown to be as much an image of God as radiant glory; in self-giving as much as in splendor, he is God's likeness. To ordinary human reason, this paradoxical icon is a puzzling presentation of divinity; it is a riddle, teasing the mind. Illogically but mystically, it points to the transforming power of God's Wisdom in death as in life.

The Christ-Riddle as Revelation in Mark

The quote from Teilhard at the beginning of the chapter speaks of our need to "disclose" God "ever more fully." Mark's gospel is structured on a similar premise. Mark presents divine mystery as a parable or riddle whose meaning is not obvious but hidden, needing to be disclosed. Above all, he dramatizes Jesus the Christ as himself the ultimate riddle of divinity hidden at the core of humanity.

In Mark, the divine disclosure also involves a transformed way of seeing—a process that further connects with Teilhard, who says, "God transforms himself as he incorporates himself into us." The peak moment of transformed perception in Mark is that of Jesus' transfiguration, a scene which, standing at the center of the narrative, discloses the divine meaning on both sides. In the first half of his gospel, Mark shows Jesus performing a series of miracles that transform not only one person's life but also the vision of those who observe them. Twice, the "crowd" is made "ecstatic"— that is, "out of their minds" with joy (2:12; 5:42). In the second and third seed parables, which provide analogies to God's kingdom, the emphasis is on the surprising transformation of the tiny seed into an unstoppable harvest or a sheltering tree. At the end of chapter 4, Jesus is disclosed to his disciples—and transformed before their eyes—into a divine presence. After Jesus dies, the meaning of his death is transformed by a Roman soldier who exclaims, "Truly this man was God's Son!" (15:39). At his tomb, the women who come to anoint him are transformed by what is disclosed to them. Like the crowds before them who witnessed transforming miracles, they are possessed by "ecstasy" (16:8a), and like the disciples silenced by Jesus' transfiguration, they are "filled with awe" (16:8b).

These series of transformations further connect Mark with Teilhard's view of transformation as God's way of creation:

"God has been creating ever since the beginning of time, and seen from within, his creation (even his initial creation?) takes the form of transformation. . . . God is continually breathing new being into us."[9]

In Mark, the disclosure of God's presence "breathes new being" into a demoniac, a mother-in-law, a leper, a sick woman, a dead little girl, a Syrophoenician mother and her daughter, a Roman soldier, and, above all, into the women who become Christ's disciples.

9. *Christianity and Evolution*, trans. René Hague (New York: Harcourt Brace, 1969), 23.

5

Matthew
God's Wisdom "Reactualized for the Present Hour"

> "It was not merely that I found no difficulty in apprehending, more or less intuitively, the organic unity of the living membrane which is stretched like a film over the lustrous surface of the star which holds us. . . . [A]n ultimate envelope was beginning to become apparent to me. . . . This envelope was not only conscious but thinking, . . . the essence or rather the very Soul of the Earth."[1]

Mark presents Christ as a person whose divinity is hidden, whose identity is secret. Even his disciples are slow to recognize who he truly is. Surprisingly, it is a Roman centurion who first grasps the paradoxical meaning of his death. Three of his disciples—Peter, James, and John—catch a glimpse of his divine identity and fall silent in awe. Three other disciples—Mary, Mary, and Salome—come to realize his transcendence of death and fall silent in awe. After the scene of his

---

1. Teilhard de Chardin, *The Heart of Matter*, 32.

transfiguration, the reader becomes aware that every scene has an added dimension to it. Beyond the obvious, Mark constantly points to another, divine reality. Matthew also undertakes to give his readers a bifocal vision, but in a different way.

Mark prefers language that is succinct, poetic, and riddling. Matthew, on the other hand, although he follows the outline of events in Mark quite closely, tends to fill in the gaps in Mark's story and spell out meanings. In particular, he names the biblical allusions that provide the bones of his story. He makes it clear, in a way that Mark does not, that the story of Jesus is based on one scriptural passage after another and serves to interpret them. Jesus is the "fulfillment of the Scriptures." This phrase does not mean (as some have suggested) that Matthew is proposing that Jesus' life was foretold or predicted by the ancient Scriptures. Rather, Matthew tries to show how Christ relives (or reactualizes) the Scriptures of Israel. The scriptural allusions that he weaves into his text provide the extra dimension, the divine reality that provides the true significance of the event.

The opening four chapters of Matthew show how this works. Matthew begins his gospel with what is ostensibly a genealogy of Jesus but on careful reflection turns out to be more symbol than history. Matthew matches Mark's opening echo of Genesis 1— "beginning"—with an echo of Genesis 2: "the book of the generations" (Gen 2:4). The parallel alerts the reader to the fact that Matthew, like the author of Genesis 2, is consciously approaching the same narrative from a different perspective. His subsequent list of ancestors is striking for its stylized division into "fourteen generations"—"from Abraham to David . . . from David to the Babylonian exile . . . from the Babylonian exile to the Messiah" (v. 17). The fact that the last segment is only thirteen generations is puzzling but does not negate Matthew's clear intent to present a symbolic narrative. In Hebrew, each letter has a numerical value; the letters in David's name add up to fourteen. Matthew, whose Jewish community was under attack from some other Jews, had reason to stress Jesus' Davidic lineage.

The second notable aspect of Matthew's genealogy is his reference to four women among Jesus' ancestors—Tamar, Rahab, Ruth, and the wife of Uriah. What is remarkable is not only the mention of women (not usually included in Jewish genealogies of the time) but the fact that each one has a story in which she at first appears to be unconventional and yet is ultimately shown to be righteous. Tamar deceives her father-in-law into lying with her and so gives birth to two sons who continue the Davidic line. Rahab is a prostitute who provides for the Israelites whom Joshua sends to scout out the promised land of Canaan. Ruth is a Gentile who stays on with her Israelite mother-in-law after her husband's death then marries another Israelite and becomes the great-grandmother of David. The wife of Uriah is wrongfully stolen from her husband by David but nonetheless becomes the mother of Solomon. By recalling these women, Matthew prepares his readers for the story of Mary, whose pregnancy out of wedlock may appear to the world to be shocking but is ultimately known to be virtuous. Matthew is setting the stage for his theme that things are not always what they seem.

In the climax of his narrative of Jesus' conception, Matthew weaves together these two symbolic strands—that is, Jesus' Davidic ancestry and God's way of reversing appearances. When Joseph is about to divorce Mary quietly (1:19), an angel of the Lord appears in a dream and, addressing him as "son of David," assures him that Mary has conceived the child "through the Holy Spirit" (1:20). Literalists have pointed out that if God is the child's father, then Joseph's relation to David is irrelevant, but Matthew is not trying to present a literal history. He is simply dramatizing what Paul proclaims at the beginning of Romans: "the gospel of God . . . the gospel concerning his Son, who was descended from David according to the flesh and was declared to be Son of God with power according to the spirit of holiness" (Rom 1:1, 3-4).

Matthew's proclamation, "she was found to be with child from the Holy Spirit" (1:18), confirms that his narrative is a spiritual document, articulating deeply symbolic (not literal) truths. Matthew clinches the point through his explicit reference to Isaiah 7:14: "Behold the virgin shall be with child and bear a son, and they shall name him Emmanuel." The word translated as "virgin" here, and in the Greek Septuagint, simply meant a young unmarried woman in the original Hebrew text and, in context, was probably referring, after the fact, to the birth of Hezekiah, the reforming king of Isaiah's time. The passage in Isaiah, in other words, was not predicting a miracle of virgin birth. It was, however, affirming that God would intervene to change the fortunes of Israel by raising up a king who would do God's will; he would be named Emmanuel—"God is with us."[2] Matthew is using the Isaiah passage to indicate that in the conception of Jesus, God has once again intervened in human history. Matthew is signaling to his readers that he is telling a spiritual story, and it has to be understood on those terms. Jesus' story is "fulfilling the Scriptures" by reliving them. The subtext here is the Jewish belief that God's power to create is ongoing and inexhaustible; as God has done before, so will God do again. Maybe Matthew was also thinking, as Mark suggests in his narrative of the blind man's cure, that God needs to communicate the same truths to nearsighted humanity more than once.

The story of the magi's visit in chapter 2 is similarly crafted to express the spiritual significance of Jesus' birth. The magi seem to be a confluence of Psalm 72, with its vision of a future king to which "the kings of Sheba and Seba bring gifts" (v. 10), and Isaiah's vision of a new Zion to which "all those from Sheba shall come. They shall bring gold and frankincense, and shall proclaim the praise of the LORD" (Isa 60:6b). Matthew probably added the third king with his gift of myrrh to indicate that Jesus' glory would be mixed with suffering.

---

2. See Raymond Brown, *The Virginal Conception and Bodily Resurrection of Christ* (New York: Paulist Press, 1973).

Matthew next tells a story that links Jesus' infancy to the story of Moses. One might speculate that the creative germ for Matthew here was the verse in Hosea referring to Israel's liberation from slavery, "Out of Egypt I have called my son" (Hos 11:1; Matt 2:15). Identifying Jesus with "the son," Matthew places Jesus in Egypt. In that context he shows that Herod is another Pharaoh, and Jesus another Moses. The contrast he is stressing is not only between oppressor and liberator but also between the wise and the foolish. It is the wisdom of the magi that is set in contrast to the ignorance of Herod. Their wisdom, like that of Balaam, is divinely inspired; like Balaam, they have seen what the Almighty sees (Num 24:16), namely, that "a star shall come out of Jacob" (Num 24:17)—that is, a person who will advance the well-being of Israel. Herod's scribes search the Jewish Scriptures for further enlightenment and respond with phrases taken from Micah: "And you, Bethlehem, in the land of Judah, are by no means least among the rulers of Judah; for from you shall come a ruler who is to shepherd my people Israel" (Mic 5:1-3; Matt 2:6). The exaltation of Bethlehem—David's birthplace—together with the image of the ruler as a "shepherd," has Davidic overtones. In Matthew's telling of the story, the prophecy frightens Herod so that he, like Pharaoh, massacres all Jewish babies under two years old. At the same time the prophecy serves as a narrative device to place Jesus and his parents in Egypt until after Herod's death—whence God can say again, "Out of Egypt I have called my son" (Hos 11:1).

The passage from Micah, like the earlier passage from Isaiah, is not a prophecy in the sense of a prediction but a reassurance that God will save his people as God has done before. Matthew uses it to suggest there is a reliable pattern to God's saving acts. He strengthens this theme by linking his narrative to the passage in Jeremiah about "Rachel weeping for her children" (Jer 31:15; Matt 2:18). In Jeremiah, the full context is a turning point for Israel; God tells Rachel to cease her mourning because "there is hope for your future: . . . your children shall come back to their own country" (Jer 31:17). Matthew similarly uses this passage as a turning point. After quoting it, he tells of Herod's death and Joseph's dream in which another angel instructs Joseph to return to the land of Israel (Matt 2:20-21). Matthew does not show Joseph returning to Bethlehem, however, but to the place tradition had long associated with the youth of Jesus—Nazareth of Galilee. He then concludes that this happened "so that what had been spoken through the prophets might be fulfilled, 'He will be called a Nazorean'" (Matt 2:23). There is in fact no such prophecy, so there have been many speculations as to why Matthew says what he does. Some have suggested that he was playing with words: perhaps Isaiah's reference to the Davidic "bud" (*neser*) from the root of Jesse (Isa 11:1), or possibly the story of Samson as one consecrated to God as a *nazir* (Judg 13). Or perhaps Matthew, wanting to stress that everything about Jesus was a reliving of the Scriptures, simply took the poetic license to invent a "prophecy."

In chapter 3, Matthew introduces John the Baptist as a new Elijah, drawing on the same scriptural references as Mark in his portrait of the prophet. Like Elijah in 2 Kings 1:8, John is dressed in camel's hair, wears a leather belt, and eats "locusts and wild honey" (Matt 3:4). Unlike Mark, however, Matthew does not relate John's preaching to past messengers to Israel. Instead, he focuses on the voice of Isaiah proclaiming "comfort" to God's people and urging them to change their hearts so as to receive it (Isa 40:1-3; Matt 3:1-3). Matthew then adapts John's preaching so that it sounds anything but comforting: "You brood of vipers! Who warned you to flee from the wrath to come? . . . Do not presume to say to yourselves, 'We have Abraham as our ancestor'; for I tell you, God is able from these stones to raise up children to Abraham. Even now the ax is lying at the root of the trees" (Matt 3:7-10).

The difference between Matthew and Mark here probably reflects the political shift effected in the decade between them: in Mark's time (immediately after the fall of the Jerusalem temple in the year 70), his Jewish-Christian community was still tolerated easily within Judaism, but by Matthew's day (around 80), Jews who were followers of Jesus were being accused by the religious establishment of not being truly Jewish. Both hurt and angered by the accusation, Matthew retaliates by having John call the Pharisees and Sadducees "a brood of vipers." This name-calling should not be taken as an accurate reflection of the role of these two religious groups in the time of Jesus. First of all, they disagreed with each other theologically: the Sadducees served the temple priests, advocated a literal reading of Scripture, and did not believe in resurrection; the Pharisees were laypeople who brought temple liturgies into ordinary homes, believed in resurrection, and developed methods for ongoing interpretation of the Bible. Many scholars think Jesus may be shown arguing with the Pharisees because he was closest to their school of thought. In any case, modern readers should keep in mind that Matthew is reflecting the complicated feelings of his own society, not the realities of the time of Jesus.

As in Mark, the relationship between John and Jesus has overtones of the relationship between Elijah and Elisha. The connection Matthew makes between John and Jesus has similar imagery to the scene in 2 Kings 2, where Elijah makes Elisha his successor—water, fire, and spirit. At the edge of the Jordan, Elisha asks for "a double portion" of Elijah's spirit (2 Kgs 2:9) and Elijah is taken up in a chariot of fire (2 Kgs 2:11). Elisha then repeats Elijah's miraculous feat of parting the waters (2 Kgs 2:14)—itself an action that reflects both God's liberating action in Exodus and God's creating act in the opening of Genesis.

There is an important difference, however, in these paired relationships. In Jewish tradition, Elijah is considered the greater prophet, even though he passed on "a double portion of his spirit" to Elisha. Here, John speaks of Jesus as the one who is "mightier" and attributes to him both "spirit and fire" (Matt 3:11). Matthew further emphasizes the difference between them by imagining a dialogue in which John at first refuses to baptize Jesus and agrees only after Jesus tells him "it is proper for us in this way to fulfill all righteousness" (3:15). The exchange confirms Matthew's concern with the theme of fulfillment; once again Matthew is stressing that Jesus is reliving the Scriptures of Israel.

In describing the baptism itself, Matthew's language follows closely the language of Mark: the opened heavens, the "Spirit of God descending like a dove," the voice from the heavens proclaiming Jesus to be, like Isaac to Abraham, God's "beloved son" (Gen 22:2). In the Old Testament, God's Holy Spirit is used interchangeably with God's Wisdom; the image of a dove recalls one of the words for the beloved in the Song of Songs; Abraham's "beloved son" is the one whom he loves the most and yet offers up to God. In using this language, both Matthew and Mark present the baptism of Jesus as a momentous turning point in the union between humanity and divinity. Jesus of Nazareth, "son of David according to the flesh," receives God's Wisdom and, through it, becomes God's "beloved." The baptism Jesus receives is not one of "repentance" but one of immersion in the Spirit.

In chapter 4 it is the Spirit that leads Jesus into the desert "to be tempted by the devil" (4:1). As Matthew constructs the temptation scene, it turns into a debate over the meaning of Scripture. The first temptation revolves around a primary speech of Moses:

> This entire commandment that I command you today you must diligently observe, so that you may live and increase, and go in and occupy the land that the LORD promised on oath to your ancestors. Remember the long way that the LORD your God has led you these forty years in the wilderness, in order to humble you, testing you to know what was in your heart, whether or not you would keep his commandments. He humbled you by letting you hunger, then by feeding you with manna, with which neither you nor your ancestors were acquainted, in order to make you understand that *one does not live by bread alone, but by every word that comes from the mouth of the* LORD. (Deut 8:1-3)

The passage in Matthew repeats all the key elements of Moses' address: Jesus, like collective Israel, fasts for forty days and nights, and, like the Israelites in the book of Exodus, he experiences hunger. The Israelites, miserable in these desert circumstances, "grumbled against Moses and Aaron," and cried out, "If only we had died by the hand of the LORD in the land of Egypt, when we sat by the fleshpots and ate our fill of bread; for you have brought us out into this wilderness to kill this whole assembly with hunger" (Exod 16:3). Matthew constructs a scene in which Jesus is also led into the desert to fast long enough to experience famine but responds differently. In this case, the devil verbalizes the temptation: "If you are the Son of God, command these stones to become loaves of bread" (4:3). Jesus' response, quoting Deuteronomy, models what every righteous person's ought to be: "One does not live by bread alone, but by every word that comes from the mouth of God" (4:4).

Jesus' response proclaims total trust in God's providence. Matthew accordingly shows the devil's second temptation to be based on this very trust. What is more, the devil quotes Psalm 91 to clinch his point. "If you are the Son of God," he says, you can throw yourself off the parapet of the temple without fear: "For it is written, 'He will command his angels concerning you,' and 'On their hands they will bear you up, so that you will not dash your foot against a stone'" (Ps 91:11-12; Matt 4:6).

The temptation here is twofold: first, to the hubris of assuming that you can do whatever you like, even to the point of taking extreme risks with your life, and God will support you; second, that you can take bits of Scripture out of context and make it serve your own purposes. These two temptations are related, of course; both are ways in which one makes oneself the reference point.

Matthew shows Jesus responding with another quote from Deuteronomy, "Do not put the Lord your God to the test" (Deut 6:16; Matt 4:7). In context, the words come again from Moses' instruction to the people to keep God's commandments and bind themselves to God's word. "Hear, O Israel," Moses says, "The LORD is our God, the LORD alone. You shall love the LORD your God with all your heart, and with all your soul, and with all your might. Keep these words that I am commanding you today in your heart" (Deut 6:4-6). And later it is written, "*Do not put the*

LORD *your God to the test*, as you tested him at Massah. You must diligently keep the commandments of the LORD your God" (Deut 6:16-17).

The reference to Massah is to the incident in Exodus 17 where the people complain to Moses because they have no water to drink, and Moses replies, "Why do you quarrel with me? Why do you test the LORD?" (Exod 17:2). The Hebrew word for "quarrel" is *meribah*, and the Hebrew word for "trial" is *massah*, and the Israelites subsequently gave these names to that place in the desert: "[Moses] called the place Massah and Meribah, because the Israelites quarreled and tested the LORD, saying, 'Is the LORD among us or not?'" (Exod 17:7). The incident, along with the names, is further memorialized in Psalm 95:

> O that today you would listen to his voice!
> > Do not harden your hearts, as at Meribah,
> > as on the day of Massah in the wilderness,
> > when your ancestors tested me,
> > and put me to the proof, though they had seen my work. (vv. 7-8)

The full context gives Jesus' terse reply robust meaning: testing God by extreme actions, it suggests, is not a sign of trust but the opposite. To understand this truth, one needs to refer to the whole of Scripture, not to a mere sound bite.

Matthew accordingly constructs the third and last temptation around the core commandment to worship God and God alone. He dramatizes the temptation against this commandment by showing the devil offering Jesus "all the kingdoms of the world" if Jesus would but worship him (Matt 4:8). Jesus responds with the very first and essential commandment, "You shall have no other gods before me" (Deut 5:7).

To sum up, Matthew dramatizes Jesus' temptations in a way that shows how Jesus relives the exodus experience, the devil tries to subvert Scripture, and Jesus responds by weaving together key passages of Moses' speech in Deuteronomy. Jesus stands for Israel in its time of trial and temptation. The temptation is not only to succumb to physical desires but to forget, misunderstand, or mis-use God's word in Scripture; Jesus resists temptation by "fulfilling" that Scripture both in word and deed.

In ancient Israel, Scripture was thought to contain the complete wisdom of God. By showing that Jesus lives out—or relives—that Scripture, Matthew indicates that Jesus' life reveals what God's wisdom looks like in the flesh. In chapter 5, Matthew shows Jesus, like Moses, teaching on a mountaintop. Like Moses, he teaches his followers how to be holy. He uses the rhetoric of blessedness, which is the language of Wisdom. The formula "Blessed are those . . ." is used in Proverbs and some of the psalms. The content is drawn largely from the psalms. "Blessed are the poor in spirit," for example, echoes the sentiment of Psalm 34, which rejoices that God always hears the cry of the poor. In Psalm 34, those in trouble are *poor in spirit*. They may or may not be materially impoverished, but they are certainly distressed, crushed, and brokenhearted. These are the very ones, the psalmist says, whom God is close to. The self-sufficient do not cry out to God; those who cry out are those who recognize their need. Their poverty then turns out to be a blessing, because God hears them and responds.

In the same vein, the second Beatitude gives assurance that God comforts those who mourn. It brings to mind many places in Scripture: the moment in Exodus when God hears his people cry (Exod 3:7); the opening of Second Isaiah, "Comfort, give comfort to my people" (Isa 40:1); God's consolation to Rachel mourning for her lost children (Jer 31:17); and, of course, God's response to Job.

The third Beatitude contains a direct quote from Psalm 37:11: "The meek shall inherit the land." In context, the psalmist sets "the meek" in direct contrast to "the wicked" who are the ones in power. "Wait a little," he exhorts (v. 10); in time, he suggests, "the wicked will be no more" (v. 10) and "the Lord upholds the righteous" (v. 17).

The Hebrew word translated as "meek" is *aniy*—a word that means, variously, "depressed in mind or circumstances, gentle, needy, afflicted, lowly, meek, poor." The range of meanings fits well with the themes of Psalm 34, Isaiah 40, Jeremiah 31, and Job (among many places in the Hebrew Scriptures). Again and again we encounter the idea that the afflicted and the needy, the lowly—the poor in spirit—will be comforted and raised up by God.

A form of this word is also used to describe Moses: "Now the man Moses was very meek [humble; NRSV], more so than anyone else on the face of the earth" (Num 12:3). Every one of these examples has a context in which the meek one is being oppressed by others who are arrogant or wicked, so that in each instance, the meek one is also a righteous person in distress. To say "the meek will inherit the earth" is to say that the wicked will *not*; ultimately, justice will be done.

The fourth Beatitude makes this idea of ultimate justice explicit: "Blessed are those who hunger and thirst for righteousness, for they will be filled" (Matt 5:6). There is an echo here of Psalm 107, "For he satisfies the thirsty, and the hungry he fills with good things" (v. 9).

There is then a shift in the Beatitudes from speaking of what God will do to restore the misfortunes of the righteous to holding up what the righteous do to please God. In the first four Beatitudes the righteous are in a passive stance, afflicted and waiting on the Lord. In the next three, they are in active mode, doing God's work. They are called blessed for being merciful, for being pure of heart, for being peacemakers (Matt 5:7-9).

These three virtues are attributes of God; those who possess them reflect God's way of being. The first is one of the very names of God:

> The Lord descended in the cloud and stood with him there, and proclaimed the name, "The Lord." The Lord passed before him, and proclaimed,
>   "The Lord, the Lord,
>   a God merciful and gracious,
>   slow to anger,
>   and abounding in steadfast love and faithfulness."
>   (Exod 34:6-7)

In Psalm 23, the psalmist concludes by saying that God's "goodness and mercy" shall follow him. Psalm 100 proclaims "his mercy is everlasting," and Psalms 106, 107, and 136 repeat, "his mercy endures forever." In Proverbs, the sage instructs his followers, "Do not let loyalty and faithfulness forsake you" (Prov 3:3) and describes the wise person as one who "pursues righteousness and kindness" (Prov 21:21).

In all these instances, the Hebrew word for "mercy" is *hesed*, which has the connotation of undeserved kindness or grace. In Exodus 34, the word for "merciful" is *rachom*, derived from *rechem* ("womb"), and implies caring for another in the way that a woman cares for the child in her womb. The pervasive sense that Scripture gives of God's maternal compassion makes the fifth Beatitude a summons to imitate it.

Those who would imitate God must first know God, must see who God is. To "see" God, one must be clear of worldly attachments. The sixth Beatitude thus follows naturally from the one before: "Blessed are the pure in heart, for they will see God" (Matt 5:8). The Hebrew word for "pure" is *bar*—derived from the verb *barar*, to clarify—and has the connotations of "clear" and "empty." In Psalm 19, a psalm praising the wisdom of God's teaching, the psalmist proclaims, "The commandment of the LORD is clear, enlightening the eyes" (v. 8). In Psalm 24, a processional psalm, the speaker asks, "Who shall ascend the hill of the LORD?" and replies, "Those who have clean hands and pure hearts" (vv. 3-4). The word translated "clean" is *naqiy*, meaning "blameless"; the "clear" is *bar*. The "pure hearts" are those who have emptied themselves of things that would distract them from God; being thus open to God, their eyes are enlightened and they "see."

Peacemaking, like mercy, is one of the core attributes of God in the Hebrew Scriptures and also a key gift that God bestows. Jews wish one another *shalom*, meaning that they wish each other God's wholeness, fullness, abundance. That meaning of peace is evident in one of the earliest priestly blessings:

The LORD bless you and keep you;
the LORD make his face to shine upon you, and be gracious
    to you;
the LORD lift up his countenance upon you, and give you
    peace [*shalom*]. (Num 6:24-26)

Isaiah sees this peace/abundance of God as key to the restoration of Zion:

How beautiful upon the mountains
    are the feet of the messenger who announces peace [*shalom*].
        (Isa 52:7)

Psalm 72 describes a king who will reflect God's wisdom, saying, "In his days may righteousness flourish and peace [*shalom*] abound, until the moon is no more" (v. 7). Psalm 37:11, which assures that the *aniy* will inherit the earth, also says they "will delight in abundant prosperity [*shalom*]." Psalm 119 celebrates God's teaching, saying, "Great peace [*shalom*] have those who love your law" (v. 165). And Proverbs links s*halom* to personified Wisdom, saying, "Her ways are ways of pleasantness, and all her paths are peace [*shalom*]" (Prov 3:17).

In summary, those who share God's compassion, God's clarity of heart, and God's wholeness are *ipso facto* blessed. External circumstances do not matter; they are blessed in their very being. Protected against external onslaught, they remain blessed in the face of persecution, insult, and false testimony (Matt 5:10-11). Grounded in God's wisdom, they can "Rejoice and be glad" (Matt 5:12).

The rest of chapter 5 shows Jesus expounding on the Law—that is, the Ten Commandments—exploring and amplifying their implications in respect to anger, adultery, divorce, oaths, and retaliation (Matt 5:21-42). His concluding instruction to "love your enemies" (Matt 5:44) is the final instruction in blessedness, a fitting coda to those Beatitudes attained by reflecting God's being: "Be perfect as your heavenly Father is perfect" (Matt 5:48).

The emphasis on wholeness and abundance is fairly straightforward in most Wisdom writings; the wise follow God's will and reap the benefits, while the wicked foolishly stray from God and are destroyed. Job, of course, challenges this neat equation, and Ecclesiastes raises questions. Matthew (and the other writers of Jesus' story) had the difficult task of linking Jesus to the wholeness and abundance of Wisdom while at the same time telling the story of his crucifixion. How to reconcile the facts of his death with their perception and presentation of him as Wisdom? His death seemed a contradiction to his life and to his promise of life. They found their way in the language of paradox. In Jesus' ultimate instruction to his disciples he tells them, "Those who find their life will lose it, and those who lose their life for my sake will find it" (Matt 10:39). Binary divisions are characteristic of Wisdom's style, but here is one on a more sophisticated level. Far from straightforward, it maintains a binary perspective while also suggesting that things may be the opposite of what they seem.

The inversion of appearance and reality means that the truth of things is often hidden; secrecy and mystery are intrinsic to the nature of paradox. This emphasis on what is hidden is central to the parables Jesus tells in Matthew 13. As in Mark, the Matthean Jesus suggests that they contain the secrets or "mysteries" of the kingdom that not everyone can understand (13:11-15) but that his disciples are "blessed" (wise) enough to see and hear (13:16).

Each parable, in turn, revolves around something hidden. In the Parable of the Weeds, when the slaves of the householder want to pull up the weeds, the householder replies, "No; for in gathering the weeds you would uproot the wheat along with them. Let both of them grow together until the harvest" (13:29-30). Anyone who farms or gardens finds this response nonsensical, but it is consistent with the larger theme of the gospel that reality is hidden from ordinary sight; what looks like a weed might turn out to be a stalk of wheat. Similarly the tiny mustard seed does not look like something that can turn into a haven for "the birds of the air" (13:32), and a bit of yeast is not obviously an ingredient that will result in risen loaves of bread (13:33).

In telling the next parable, Jesus makes explicit what is implied in the former three: namely, that the kingdom of heaven is not obvious but hidden. It is like "treasure hidden in a field" (13:44). It is not something we can see right away, but the object of continual search—"like a merchant in search of fine pearls" (13:45).

The final parable clarifies the one on the weeds because just as the weeds and the wheat grow together, so here the net of the kingdom has a broad and indiscriminate reach: "The kingdom of heaven is like a net that was thrown into the sea and caught fish of every kind" (13:47). If there is to be a sorting out, it is to be done by angels at the end of time (13:48-50).

This theme of the hidden kingdom fits well with the rabbinic idea that all of God's revelation is hidden in the Bible; that was why they saw it as "a religious task" for each faith community to keep reopening the Scriptures to search for new meanings. Near the end of chapter 13, Matthew makes this connection explicit: "Therefore every scribe [that is, Scripture scholar] who has been trained for the kingdom of heaven is like the master of a household who brings out of his treasure what is new and what is old" (13:52).

At the very conclusion of the chapter, Matthew places the scene of Jesus' rejection in his hometown, thereby extending the theme of hidden truth to the identity of Jesus. His wording here (Matt 13:54-58) is almost identical with that of Mark (6:1-6). The only difference lies in the way each writer contextualizes the moment. Mark does so by showing Jesus repeatedly telling others (demons as well as humans) not to reveal his identity; Matthew does so by making this incident the climax to a series of parables about hidden truth. So each, in his different way, sets up a pattern of purposeful secrecy. Both suggest that one needs God's eyes to discern the kingdom of heaven, to uncover the meaning of the Scriptures, to perceive God's Wisdom in a crucified messiah.

"Christ crucified," Paul says, is "a stumbling block to Jews and foolishness to Gentiles, but to those who are the called, both Jews and Greeks, Christ the power of God and the wisdom of God" (1 Cor 1:23-24). Matthew, like Mark, dramatizes the truth of Paul's observation in the narrative of Peter. When Jesus asks, "Who do you say that I am?" (Mark 8:29; Matt 16:15), Peter first replies, "You are the messiah" (Mark 8:29; Matt 16:16). Matthew adds to Peter's response, "You are the son of the living God" (16:16). In Matthew's narrative, Jesus then commends Peter for his insight and proclaims him the "rock" on which he will build his church (16:17-19). Matthew goes on, however, as Mark does, to show that Peter's understanding of Jesus' identity is limited. When Jesus speaks of his suffering and death, Peter cannot fit that into his understanding of a messiah. Matthew and Mark use identical words to describe this: "Peter took him [Jesus] aside and began to rebuke him" (Mark 8:32; Matt 16:22a). Matthew adds the words of that rebuke: "God forbid it, Lord! This must never happen to you" (16:22b). Peter, it is implied, associated a "messiah" with power; he could not connect the term with suffering and death. For him, a crucified messiah would be an oxymoron, a "stumbling block" and "foolishness." Jesus' response to Peter is sharply clarifying: "Get behind me, Satan! . . . You are setting your mind not on divine things but on human things" (Mark 8:33; Matt 16:23). It will take Peter longer to "see" as God does, to understand the paradox of "Christ crucified" as the wisdom of God.

The paradox of death and resurrection is the core of a whole web of paradoxical teachings in Matthew. In chapter 18, for example, Jesus teaches that the greatest in the kingdom will be those who have "become like children" (18:2). Jesus relates this to the virtue of humility: "Whoever becomes humble like this child is the greatest in the kingdom of heaven" (18:4). Jesus' meaning here must be put into the larger context of his emphasis on the needy. In any society, children have needs they cannot fulfill by themselves; they are inherently dependent and, in that sense, are "poor in spirit." In holding up a child as a model for adults, Jesus again suggests, as he does in the first Beatitude, the blessedness of recognizing one's need for God.

Jesus teaches a similar reversal of conventional attitudes when he speaks about the rich and poor. When approached by the rich young man who has kept all the commandments and asks, "What do I still lack?" (19:20), Jesus replies, "If you wish to be perfect, go, sell your possessions, and give the money to the poor, and you will have treasure in heaven; then come, follow me" (19:21). The disciples, "greatly astonished," ask, "Then who can be saved?" (19:25). It is natural for human beings to think that human fortune is a sign of divine favor; the opposite is a paradox that is hard to take. Jesus' response here acknowledges the difficulty: "For mortals it is impossible, but for God all things are possible" (19:26). As Jesus distinguishes, in his reproach to Peter, between seeing as human beings see and as God sees, so here he distinguishes between what human beings can do and what God can do. To share in God's power, God's life (to be "perfect"), human beings are called not only to see with God's paradoxical perspective but to live it. "Losing one's life to save it" means choosing to be needy.

The third paradox involves power. The mother of James and John, seeking greatness for her sons (a normal maternal desire), asks of Jesus, "Declare that these two sons of mine will sit, one at your right hand and one at your left, in your kingdom" (20:21). Jesus teaches that they should seek the opposite:

> You know that the rulers of the Gentiles lord it over them, and their great ones are tyrants over them. It will not be so among you; but whoever wishes to be great among you must be your servant, and whoever wishes to be first among you must be your slave; just as the son of man came not to be served but to serve, and to give his life a ransom for many. (20:25-28)

In the last verse Jesus offers himself as a model; he is the living paradox he calls his disciples to emulate. Matthew, by having Jesus refer to himself as "son of man," indicates that he sees Jesus as representative humanity. By the phrase, "a ransom for many," Matthew further links Jesus to Isaiah's Suffering Servant, whom God commends for sacrificing his life for others (Isa 53:12). All of these teachings are preparatory in Matthew to his account of how Jesus' final days of arrest, trial, suffering, and death lead to his resurrection and glory. In these final chapters, language and content fuse; the rhetoric of paradox blossoms into the paradoxical meaning of the cross, where death is the way to life.

In describing Jesus' crucifixion, Matthew follows Mark's plot line quite closely, but he frames each moment with a scriptural quote or allusion. As in Mark, Matthew's description of Jesus' anointing by a woman foreshadows Jesus' words and gestures at his last supper. In both Mark and Matthew, the verb to describe the woman's action is "pour out" (Mark 14:3; Matt 26:7); in both accounts, Jesus identifies the wine he offers his disciples as his blood "poured out" (Mark 14:24; Matt 26:28). The verb (*ekxew*) indicates an extravagant spilling forth. It is used in Joel to describe the pouring out of God's Spirit in the final days: "I will *pour out* my spirit on all flesh" (Joel 2:28-29). It is also used in Isaiah to explain the ultimate exaltation of God's Suffering Servant:

> Therefore I will allot him a portion with the great . . .
> because he *poured out* himself to death. (Isa 53:12)

The woman pours out the ointment as Jesus pours out the wine, as he will pour out his blood. She has anticipated the gesture that symbolizes his death. As Jesus says, she has prepared him for burial (26:12). At the same time, she has anointed not his feet, as was the custom for burial, but his head—the customary manner of anointing kings. She has, in effect, made him *a messiah*, one anointed for God's work. In Matthew's narrative as in Mark's, her action is a prophetic sign that Jesus' death is paradoxically also a blessing. That is why Jesus can say, as he does in both these gospels, "Wherever this good news is proclaimed in the whole world, what she has done will be told in remembrance of her" (Mark 14:9; Matt 26:13).

Matthew augments Mark's account of Judas's betrayal of Jesus with the detail, "They paid him thirty pieces of silver" (26:15). Though slight, the addition evokes three places in Scripture: Exodus 21:32, where that amount is the price of a slave; Zechariah 11:12-13, where that amount represents the wages of a shepherd; and possibly, Genesis 37:28, where twenty pieces (instead of thirty) is given as the price paid for Joseph.

In his description of Jesus' last supper, Matthew adds the further detail of Jesus predicting his betrayer: "He who has dipped his hand into the bowl with me will betray me" (26:23). His observation fits the literal context, but it also echoes Psalm 41, "Even my bosom friend in whom I trusted, who ate of my bread, has lifted the heel against me" (v. 9).

We know that Matthew intends these details to be scriptural echoes because he quotes Jesus saying right after that, "The [s]on of [m]an goes *as it is written* of him" (26:24), and again a few verses later: "You will all become deserters because of me this night; *for it is written*: 'I will strike the shepherd, and the sheep of the flock will be scattered'" (Matt 26:31; see Zech 13:7).

Matthew weaves these scriptural threads into his narrative to show that not just what Jesus does but also everything that happens to him is a reliving of the Scriptures; he wants his readers to understand the sufferings of Jesus in their light.

This emphasis comes to a head when Judas comes with a group to arrest Jesus and "one of those with Jesus" cuts off the ear of someone in the arresting party (26:51). In rebuking his violence, the Matthean Jesus adds, "Do you think that I cannot appeal to my Father, and he will at once send me more than twelve legions of angels? But how then would the scriptures be fulfilled, which say it must happen in this way? . . . But all this has taken place, so that the scriptures of the prophets may be fulfilled" (26:53, 56). As in the baptism scene, Matthew shows Jesus stepping outside his story, as it were, to comment on the reason for the narrative.

Matthew goes on to describe the burial of Judas in a potter's field as a fulfillment of the Scriptures. Although what biblical verses he had in mind are unclear, his intention is not:

> Then was fulfilled what had been spoken through the prophet Jeremiah, "And they took the thirty pieces of silver, the price of the one on whom a price had been set, on whom some of the people of Israel had set a price, and they gave them for the potter's field." (Matt 27:9-10)

The silence of Jesus before Pilate is a reliving of the Suffering Servant's silence before his accusers (Isa 53:7). The Roman soldiers' mockery of Jesus also echoes the torment of the Servant:

> I gave my back to those who struck me,
>   and my cheeks to those who pulled out the beard;
> I did not hide my face
>   from insult and spitting. (Isa 50:6)

As in Mark, details of the crucifixion come right from the Psalms. The mixing of wine with vinegar that is offered to Jesus (see Mark 15:23; Matt 27:34) recalls Psalm 69:20-21:

> Insults have broken my heart,
>   so that I am in despair.
> I looked for pity, but there was none;
>   and for comforters, but I found none.
> They gave me poison for food,
>   and for my thirst they gave me vinegar to drink.

The dividing of Jesus' clothes (see Mark 15:24; Matt 27:35) is a gesture that repeats the imagery of Psalm 22:18-19:

> They stare and gloat over me;
> they divide my clothes among themselves;
>   and for my clothing they cast lots.

The passersby who shake their heads at Jesus (Mark 15:29; Matt 27:39) recall Psalm 22 and the book of Lamentations:

> All who see me mock at me;
>> they make mouths at me, they shake their heads. (Ps 22:7)

> All who pass along the way
>> clap their hands at you;
> they hiss and wag their heads. (Lam 2:15)

Like Mark, Matthew echoes the comments of "the wicked" about the righteous one in the Wisdom of Solomon:

> Let us test him with insult and torture,
> so that we may find out how gentle he is,
> and make trial of his forbearance. (Wis 2:19)

Like Mark, Matthew also draws on the way "the wicked" observe that the righteous one "calls himself a child of the Lord" (Wis 2:13) and "boasts that God is his father" (Wis 2:16). So, they reason, let God protect him. Mark describes the soldiers' mockery but does not make an explicit connection to the wicked plotters of Wisdom. Matthew, however, makes this link clear. In his version of events, the mockers say, "He trusts in God; let God deliver him now, if he wants to; for he said, 'I am God's Son'" (27:43).

At the moment of Jesus' death, both Mark and Matthew place on Jesus' lips the opening words of Psalm 22: "My God, my God, why have you abandoned me?" In Mark, the address to God is quoted in Aramaic, while in Matthew it is given in Hebrew, but both use these words as an appropriate way to express the position of Jesus in extremis. To understand their significance it is necessary to understand their context. The speaker of Psalm 22 begins in apparent despair, but he ends praising God who has saved him. Within itself the psalm contains a dramatic shift from despair to rejoicing, one that parallels Jesus' shift from death to resurrection. A Jewish audience familiar with the whole psalm would have heard, in that opening verse, the reverse ending to come. But the mocking bystanders, ever obtuse to scriptural reference, mistake "Eli" ("my God") for Elijah (27:47).

The "Divine Milieu" of Matthew's Narrative

Matthew's account of Jesus' death is a tapestry of scriptural allusions, indicating that what is happening is not to be viewed through human eyes only but seen through God's. In that alternate reality, Jesus is not a human disgrace but a glorious "fulfillment" (a reliving) of God's word. The reader is expected to keep both levels of meaning in mind and to interpret the literal happening in terms of the symbolic significance that Scripture would accord it.

Matthew's bifocal vision provides a concrete dramatization of Teilhard's idea of a "film" or "envelope" of meaning that stretches over the earth and all earthly activity, giving human life (both actions and suffering) a divine dimension of reality. It is a dimension of "conscious thinking" that offers for contemplation "the very Soul of the Earth."

6

Luke

God's Spirit (Wisdom) as the Divine Energy Creating the Future

"In other words, a second species of Spirit was emerging—and this species was no longer above our heads—it lay transversely, appearing, we might say, on the horizon."[1]

"It was a God of the Ahead who had suddenly appeared athwart the God of the Above, so that henceforth we can no longer worship fully unless we superimpose those two images so that they form one."[2]

In Mark, God's truth is hidden and has to be unwrapped or discovered. In Matthew, divine reality surrounds human reality but becomes visible only when viewed through the lens of Scripture. Luke strives to present the human and divine dimensions together, holistically. He presents divine action as human history, uniting these two levels as cause and effect. Central to

1. Teilhard de Chardin, *The Heart of Matter*, 45.
2. *Heart of Matter*, 53.

his vision is the idea of God's Spirit as the animating force of human events, driving them forward.

Luke's way of telling the story of Christ brings his Greco-Roman belief in the principle of cause and effect together with his attraction to the Jewish proclamation of God's surprising interventions. This uniting of cultures undoubtedly also influences Luke's thematic emphasis on the universality of Christ as well as his style, which mimics both the Greco-Roman and the biblical ways of presenting history.

The difference between Luke and the other evangelists is evident from his very first paragraph. Most striking, Luke does not begin with either an echo or reference to Scripture. Instead, he speaks of arranging a narrative that had been "handed down" (1:2). The word translated "handed down" recalls Paul's account of Jesus' last supper—"I received from the Lord what I also handed on to you" (1 Cor 11:23)—and indicates that although Luke speaks of "eyewitnesses" (1:2), he is not one of them; like Paul, he is passing on what he has received. His emphasis, however, is not on just repeating what he has heard but on telling it differently. His aim is to "investigate everything carefully from the very first" and then to put it in "an orderly account" (1:3). The implication is that the past versions of the story, put forward by the many who have undertaken to compile it (1:1), are untidy, and Luke finds an untidy account less compelling. He has decided to redo it so that his religious reader (Theophilus, lover of God) might feel secure or certain about what he has been taught.

The mention of "eyewitnesses" and the emphasis on "investigating," "accuracy," and "certainty" are the language of the historian, not the poet or storyteller or philosopher. The passion for order is also representative of the Greco-Roman writing of the time, not the Jewish biblical writing that thrived on paradox, surprise, and the juxtaposition of opposites. What was "foolishness to the Gentiles" could be wit and wisdom to the Jews and vice versa. So Luke rewrites the Jesus narrative in a different framework from the others and begins not with a poetic or philosophic reference to "the

Word made flesh," and strikingly not with a biblical context, but with the seeming history of the two chief protagonists, John and Jesus, and the historical context of "King Herod of Judea" (1:5).

Particularly notable in comparing Luke to the other gospels is the way he uses the words "fulfilled," "beginning," and "word." He describes his forthcoming narrative as one of "things fulfilled among us," but unlike Mark and Matthew, he seems to imply a prophecy come true, not God's ancient word being relived or "re-actualized" in the present.

Similarly, the word "beginning" (*archē*) has an entirely different connotation here than in Mark or John. Here it carries no suggestion of either Creation or Wisdom; it simply refers to the beginning of the story—the historical beginning according to "eyewitnesses."

Most significant of all, *logos* does not have the same overtones in Luke of a hypostasized attribute of God or a divine agent. "Word" here is not a persona but simply speech. When Luke speaks of the "servants of the word" (v. 2), the reference is simply to those who passed on the Jesus story. At the end of his opening sentence, Luke does not even refer to "the word" but speaks of "words" that he would like to verify for his reader. There is no sense here of the Jewish tradition of God creating by his Word, or of "the Word made flesh," or of a mystical aura attached to God's Word. Coming from a Greco-Roman culture, Luke finds it more seemly to speak of the order and accuracy of words; he will arrange them afresh so that the reader will feel they present a compelling truth.

All of this emphasis leads the reader to expect a historical account. What follows in chapters 1 and 2, however, is a highly stylized narrative in which angels appear and various persons "filled with the Spirit" burst into song or prophecy. These spiritual events are ordered sequentially so as to present the semblance of history, but they are also arranged carefully in balanced pairs; the overall effect is one of architectural design.

Within these formal structures, Luke constructs scenes that imitate ones found in the Old Testament and uses phrases that, while not strictly allusions to Old Testament passages, have an

Old Testament flavor. In Genesis, for example, when God forms a covenant with Abraham, he asks him to be "blameless" (Gen 17:1). Job is also described as "blameless" (Job 1:1), and the opening verse of Psalm 119 praises the one who is "blameless." Here, Luke speaks of both Zechariah and Elizabeth living "blamelessly" (Luke 1:6). Elizabeth is like Sarah in being "barren" and "getting on in years" (Luke 1:7). The angel announcing the birth of John appears to Zechariah when "the whole assembly of the people was praying" (Luke 1:10)—language that echoes the instruction to slaughter the Passover lamb "when the whole assembly of Israel" is present (Exod 12:6). The angel's description of John's consecrated abstemiousness—"He must never drink wine or strong drink" (Luke 1:15)—echoes the instructions the angel gives to Samson's mother as preparation for her consecrated son: "Be careful not to drink wine or strong drink" (Judg 13:4). Zechariah's punishment of speechlessness for questioning the angel (Luke 1:19-20) seems arbitrary and harsh, but no more so than that of Moses for striking the rock twice for water (Num 20:11-12).

The angel Gabriel's announcement to Mary of the birth of Jesus follows a pattern similar to the announcement given to Zechariah, while the language echoes that of God promising David a kingdom. In 2 Samuel, God tells David, "Your house and your kingdom shall be made sure forever before me" (2 Sam 7:16). In Luke, Gabriel tells Mary, "[T]he Lord God will give to him the throne of his ancestor David. . . . [A]nd of his kingdom there will be no end" (Luke 1:32-33).

Mary's canticle of thanksgiving for her child is modeled closely on Hannah's song of thanksgiving for Samuel (1 Sam 2:1-10; Luke 1:46-55); both women set their praise of God in the larger context of God's care for the poor and lowly. Zechariah's parallel canticle of thanksgiving for the birth of John does not echo any particular psalm but uses phrases that remind us of many of the psalms: praising God for "visiting" his people, for "raising up a horn" for our salvation, for "promising" salvation, for being "mindful" of his covenant (Luke 1:67-72). The description of John as a prophet who "will go before the Lord to prepare his ways" (Luke 1:76) echoes the words describing the second coming of Elijah in Malachi 3:1. These words from Malachi are quoted directly in Matthew 11:10; here, they are part of a whole piece that imitates the sound and texture of Old Testament prophecy.

Luke's writing style is characterized by *mimesis* rather than by intertextuality. The difference is subtle but important. Intertextuality occurs when a writer weaves quotes and allusions into a work in order to recall another work. The quotes or allusions offer an interpretive context for the writer's immediate piece; they are a shortcut to meaning. *Mimesis*, on the other hand, occurs when the writer tries to imitate a style in a general way. The imitation serves to place the writer's work in a tradition or school of writing but it does not illuminate a specific work or use one work to interpret another. As we have seen, Mark and Matthew are intertextual writers; they rely heavily on scriptural quotes and allusion to interpret the story of Jesus. Luke does not use Scripture for interpretive purposes but rather mimics Old Testament language in order to give his narrative the atmosphere or ethos of ancient Scripture.

At the same time that Luke imitates Old Testament writing, he also imitates the style and syntax of Greco-Roman history. The openings of both chapter 1 and chapter 2 are good examples. Addressing Theophilus in his prologue (1:1-3), Luke imitates the way Greco-Roman historians typically dedicated their work to a patron. In his opening to chapter 2, Luke imitates their formal way of setting their story in a historical context:

> In those days a decree went out from Emperor Augustus that the whole world should be registered. This was the first registration and was taken while Quirinius was governor of Syria. All went to their own towns to be registered. Joseph also went from the town of Nazareth in Galilee to Judea, to the city of David called Bethlehem, because he was descended from the house and family of David. He went to be registered with Mary, to whom he was engaged and who was expecting a child. (2:1-5)

Scholars who have explored the historical references here have found that the facts do not correspond with Luke's account: there is simply no record of such a universal census under Caesar Augustus or anyone else. But Luke's style lends the claim historical flavor, just as his psalm-like phrases in chapter 1 give his narrative a scriptural aura.

The history-like narrative allows Luke to proclaim that Jesus is of Davidic descent as if it were fact. It is instructive to see how different Luke is from Matthew in making the same theological point. As we have seen, Matthew introduces Jesus by means of a largely symbolic genealogy, which emphasizes a Davidic framework, ancestral mothers as well as fathers, and God's way of reversing appearances. His story of Joseph's dilemma emphasizes the difference between human perception of reality and the divine understanding of it, and he interprets the significance of Jesus' conception through a verse from Isaiah. Luke omits any suggestion of embarrassment or awkwardness about Mary's pregnancy, along with any scriptural precedents or symbolic interpretations. As one who wants to set his story in history, he is more concerned with how "Jesus of Nazareth" could have been born in Bethlehem of Judea; he accordingly sets forth the plausible tale of a census to account for it. In addition, the description of the census as one that involved "the whole world" is in line with his theological theme of Jesus' universality.

Luke continues to emphasize this universality in his narrative of events following Jesus' birth. Instead of Matthew's scripturally inspired story of gift-bearing kings and his reliving of Pharaoh's massacre of Jewish infants, Luke speaks of an infant wrapped in swaddling clothes and lying in a manger (2:7, 12, 16), worshiped by angels singing of peace (2:13-14) and poor shepherds "glorifying and praising God" (2:20). Matthew emphasizes Jesus' connection to God's promise to David and God's rescue of Israel; Luke emphasizes how Jesus' birth brings with it the promise of peace for common humanity. The census of Caesar Augustus is shown to have further significance: the subtext here is *Pax Christi* versus *Pax Romana*.

The subsequent narrative about Jesus' circumcision and presentation in the temple briefly offers a Jewish context for Jesus' infancy. Here, Luke stresses that Jesus' beginnings were in accordance with Jewish law: "After eight days had passed, it was time to circumcise the child; and he was called Jesus" (2:21); "When the time came for their purification according to the law of Moses, they [his parents] brought him up to Jerusalem to present him to the Lord" (2:22). As many others have pointed out, Luke's knowledge of Jewish law was sketchy: the "purification" ritual was only for the mother, and it did not usually involve presentation in the temple. But Luke had another point to make, namely, how what had begun within Judaism had expanded to universal significance. Luke proclaims this through the words of Simeon: "[M]y eyes have seen your salvation, which you have prepared in the presence of all peoples, a light for revelation to the Gentiles" (2:29-32).

Here, Luke is quoting from the second song of Isaiah's Suffering Servant when he comes to realize that God is calling him to a wider vocation than the saving of Israel:

> It is too light a thing that you should be my servant
>> to raise up the tribes of Jacob
>> and to restore the survivors of Israel;
> I will give you as a light to the nations,
>> that my salvation may reach to the end of the earth. (Isa 49:6)

It is striking that one of the few passages from Scripture that Luke quotes directly is one that speaks of Israel's universal mission. He plucks out of Jesus' Jewish context one place that indicates that in favoring Israel, God had the whole world in mind.

Luke deepens this theme of God's inclusiveness in his narrative of Jesus lost and found in the temple (2:41-52). In many ways, the story adumbrates the narrative of Jesus' death and resurrection. Jesus goes to Jerusalem for the Feast of Passover; Jesus is seemingly lost to his family, who look for him "in great anxiety"; Jesus is then found, but in a new role—no longer child but teacher in his "Father's house," astounding "all who heard him." The narrative also suggests that Jesus outgrew his natural family and shifted from being a worshiper in the temple to being its chief rabbi.

Luke's subsequent handling of the story of Jesus' baptism picks selectively from the accounts in Mark and Matthew and then expands on them in ways that continue his theme of Jesus' universality. Like Mark, he says that John preached "a baptism of repentance for the forgiveness of sins" (Luke 3:3; Mark 1:4). Unlike both Mark and Matthew, however, he makes no comparison between John and Elijah, and when he quotes Isaiah as they did, he extends the quote until it reaches a climax relevant to all people: "All flesh shall see the salvation of God" (Luke 3:6; Isa 40:5). He repeats the same warning words to Jews that Matthew attributes to John ("You brood of vipers," etc.) but then goes on to imagine John giving specific instruction to a wider audience in the form of three types of listeners—"the crowds," "tax collectors," and "soldiers" (Luke 3:7-14). Luke replaces Matthew's "Pharisees and Sadducees" (Matt 3:7) with generic "crowds"; he then adds "soldiers," thereby including even the Romans. In Mark and Matthew, John speaks mysteriously about the identity of Jesus, saying that "one is coming after" him who is "mightier" than he (Mark 1:7; Matt 3:11). Luke reduces the matter of Jesus' identity from a general mystery to a specific question: "[A]ll were questioning in their hearts concerning John, whether he might be the Messiah" (3:15).

Luke concludes the chapter by giving the genealogy of Jesus in reverse order from that of Matthew. Instead of tracing Jesus' ancestry forward from Abraham to David to the exile to the Messiah (Matt 1:1-17), Luke traces his lineage back to Adam, the universal human ancestor, whom he names "son of God" (3:23-37). In striving to write down events "in an orderly sequence," Luke has chosen a different order of priorities than either Mark or Matthew.

Speech in these opening chapters is markedly formal, mimicking both biblical and Greco-Roman styles. Gabriel's speeches to both

Zechariah and Mary are constructed carefully with parallel phrases: "Do not be afraid" (1:13 and 1:30); "you will bear a son and you will name him . . ." (1:13 and 1:31); "he will be great" (1:15 and 1:32). Both Mary and Zechariah respond to the births of their children with formal canticles of praise modeled on the psalms (1:46-55; 1:68-79). The angel who announces the birth of Jesus to the shepherds repeats the formal language of the earlier birth announcements: "Do not be afraid, for behold I proclaim to you . . ." (2:10). The angels burst into psalm-like song (2:14). Even the shepherds speak in a formal way: "Let us go now to Bethlehem and see this thing that has taken place, which the Lord has made known to us" (2:15). Simeon, too, speaks in biblical cadences (2:29-32).

In chapter 3, John's preaching, which appears fiery in Matthew, is organized and interpreted by Luke as ethical instruction (3:10-14)—the kind of sermon more congenial to the Greeks and the Romans than the mystical aspirations of the Jews.

In chapter 4, Luke retells Matthew's account of Jesus' temptation almost verbatim. The main difference is in the ordering of the material: Luke places the temptation to worldly power second rather than last and makes the climax the temptation to test God by jumping off the parapet of the Jerusalem temple. Luke's retelling of Matthew's account shows no interest in biblical interpretation. Rather, the reordering seems to reflect Luke's sense of moral priorities by showing how temptation starts with personal comfort, then comprises "the kingdoms of the world," and finally moves to the hubris of challenging God. The reordering also suits the structure of Luke's narrative, which links Jesus' ultimate mission to his acceptance of death in Jerusalem.

Luke's story of Jesus' rejection in his hometown is more elaborate than in Mark or Matthew. Both of these earlier evangelists tell the story as a dramatization of the proverb, "A prophet is not without honor except in his native place" (Mark 6:4, Matt 13:57); their emphasis is on the misleading human tendency to associate the divine with the spectacular. Luke instead tells a story that gives a specific historical reason for the townsfolk's rejection of their

prophet. Mark and Matthew simply say Jesus taught in the synagogue at Nazareth; Luke projects what he might have said. He
imagines him reading from the scroll of Isaiah:

> The Spirit of the Lord is upon me,
>> because he has anointed me to bring good news to the poor.
> He has sent me to proclaim release to the captives
>> and recovery of sight to the blind, to let the oppressed go free,
> to proclaim the year of the Lord's favor. (Isa 61:1-2)

The passage is not considered messianic by modern Jews, but
there is evidence that it was interpreted that way by the Essenes
and so may have been read as such by Luke.[3] In any case, Luke
uses it to proclaim his own understanding of Jesus: he shows Jesus
saying, "Today this scripture has been fulfilled in your hearing"
(4:21).

Although it may seem that Luke is speaking of "fulfillment of
the scriptures" in the same way as Matthew, a close look shows he
is not. In Matthew, every allusion to the Scriptures is accompanied
by a narrative in which Jesus relives a particular passage or story
in the Old Testament. In Luke, the Scripture passage is not tied
to any specific action on the part of Jesus; it is a general proclamation of his mission.

"Fulfillment" does not mean for Luke, as it does for Matthew,
the reliving of an ancient scriptural word; it means the coming
true of a prophecy. The implication here is that Jesus reads the
Isaiah text as the prediction of a particular future messiah and that
he then proclaims himself to be that one. Luke, a Gentile, set this

---

3. See *The Jewish Study Bible*, ed. Adele Berlin and Marc Zvi Brettler,
which says the speaker here is either Zion itself or the prophet (New York:
Oxford University Press, 2004), 905. On the other hand, *The Jewish Annotated
New Testament*, ed. Amy-Jill Levine and Marc Zvi Brettler (New York:
Oxford University Press, 2011), 106, speaks of messianic interpretations in
Qumran texts 1QH 14.14 and 11QMelch 1.18.

reading tradition for the Gentile church that followed in the second century—and for centuries thereafter. Yet it is important for modern Christians to understand that in first-century Judaism, this way of understanding prophecy and fulfillment would not have been a common one. In Jesus' own community, the prophet did not predict the future but gave voice to the perspective of God. That voice might warn of dire consequences if God's will was not obeyed, or project a vision of happy rewards if God's will was heeded, but neither warning nor vision was prediction. At times, the prophetic voice spoke to offer an explanation after the fact (Jeremiah, for example, was probably preaching to the exiles), but such preaching was reflecting on past events, not foretelling future ones. Luke's understanding of both scriptural prophecy and scriptural fulfillment owes more to Greek understanding of the fateful predictions of oracles than to the Jewish understanding of the prophet as the mouthpiece of God.

In any event, as Luke tells the story, Jesus' proclamation that he himself is the fulfillment of the passage from Isaiah does not disturb the worshipers in the synagogue. On the contrary, "All spoke well of him and were amazed at the gracious words that came from his mouth" (4:22). But then Luke elaborates on the narrative of Mark and Matthew to suggest that Jesus added some deliberately provocative words.

> But the truth is, there were many widows in Israel in the time of Elijah, when the heaven was shut up three years and six months, and there was a severe famine spread over all the land; yet Elijah was sent to none of them except to a widow at Zarephath in Sidon. There were also many lepers in Israel in the time of Elisha, and none of them was cleansed except Naaman the Syrian. (4:25-27)

In Mark and Matthew, Jesus' townsfolk simply question how one of their own could perform miracles, but in Luke, Jesus goes out of his way to point out to them that God has often sent his prophets outside of Israel. Luke sets the stage for the people's anger at Jesus: "When they heard this, all in the synagogue were filled with rage" (4:28). The scene is in keeping with Luke's desire to bolster the confidence of the Gentiles; he wants his Gentile audience to know that Jesus' mission is also to them.

In chapter 5, Luke presents Jesus' call of Peter in ways that echo the call of Isaiah. The scene seems to start as an ordinary fishing venture. Then Jesus uses Simon Peter's boat as a preaching pulpit and afterwards says to him, "Put out into the deep water and let down your nets for a catch" (5:4). Peter first objects, "Master, we have worked all night long but have caught nothing," but then acquiesces, "Yet if you say so, I will let down the nets" (5:5). This time the nets are filled to the point of tearing and the boats are filled to the point of sinking (5:6-7). Peter's reaction is like that of Isaiah to the seraphim crying "Holy, holy, holy!" (Isa 6:2-3). Isaiah, overwhelmed by God's sacred presence, wants to escape from it: "And I said: 'Woe is me! I am lost, for I am a man of unclean lips, and I live among a people of unclean lips; yet my eyes have seen the King, the LORD of hosts!'" (Isa 6:5). In a similar way, Peter finds the divine presence too much for him: "When Simon Peter saw it, he fell down at Jesus' knees, saying, 'Go away from me, Lord, for I am a sinful man'" (Luke 5:8). An angel reassures Isaiah, and God sends him off as his prophet (Isa 6:6-8); Jesus reassures Peter and gives him the universal mission to "catch human beings" (Luke 5:10).

Here is one instance, incidentally, in which Luke does show Scripture being relived but he does not label it as a "fulfillment of the Scriptures" because, as we have seen, that concept means for him a prophecy come true, not God's word revitalized. So he makes use of the Isaiah story as he makes use of Hannah's song, to give his narrative the aura of ancient Scripture.

In general, Luke's gospel differs from the others both because of his attitude towards Scripture and because it is laid out in an orderly sequence, as a narrative of cause and effect. These stylistic differences are related to other key differences in Luke: his understanding of "messiah," his limited use of Wisdom rhetoric, and his expanded emphasis on God's "Holy Spirit."

Luke's Understanding of "Messiah"

An examination of Luke's use of the word "messiah" shows that he understood the term differently than Mark or Matthew. For them, the term held the meaning common in first-century Judaism of *the anointed one*—that is, one anointed to do God's work. It is a term that is used thirty-eight times in the Old Testament, where it is applied to a wide range of people, from kings to priests to prophets. Isaiah even applies it to Cyrus of Persia because he allowed the Jews to return from Babylon to Jerusalem and rebuild their temple (Isa 45:1). In the scrolls of Qumran, there is expectation of two messiahs: one a king, the other a priest. In 1990, a symposium of scholars from all over the world concluded:

> There was no single, discernible role description of a "Messiah" into which a historical figure like Jesus could be fit. Rather, each group which entertained a messianic hope interpreted "Messiah" in light of its historical experiences and reinterpreted Scripture accordingly.[4]

So where do modern Christians get the idea that all Jews of that time were yearning for a single messiah and then missed him when he came? Probably they receive that understanding from the Gospel of Luke.

4. *The Messiah: Developments in Earliest Judaism and Christianity*, ed. James H. Charlesworth, James Brownson, M.T. Davis, Steven J. Kraftchick, and Alan Segal (Minneapolis: Fortress Press, 1992), xv. Similar findings can be found in *Judaisms and Their Messiahs at the Turn of the Christian Era*, ed. Jacob Neusner, William Scott Green, and Ernest S. Frerichs (Cambridge: Cambridge University Press, 1987).

First of all, Luke has the angels announce this explicitly to the shepherds outside of Bethlehem: "[T]o you is born this day in the city of David a Savior, who is the Messiah, the Lord" (2:11). Matthew's magi simply inquire, "Where is the child who has been born king of the Jews?" (Matt 2:2), and Herod translates that into "where the Messiah was to be born" (Matt 2:4). Matthew, like Mark, then shows that the term was misunderstood by Peter, who is rebuked by Jesus when he cannot reconcile it with the idea of Jesus' death (Mark 8:31-33; Matt 16:21-23).

Mark and Matthew point to the paradox of the term when it is applied to one who is crucified. Luke does not seem to see the problem. On the road to Emmaus, he puts this speech into the mouth of Jesus:

> "Oh, how foolish you are, and how slow of heart to believe all that the prophets have declared! Was it not necessary that the Messiah should suffer these things and then enter into his glory?" Then beginning with Moses and all the prophets, he interpreted to them the things about himself in all the scriptures. (24:25-27)

The passage implies that the Old Testament is filled with references to a suffering messiah. But, in fact, there are none. The thirty-eight allusions to a messiah are to someone who shared God's glory, not to someone who was put to death. The Qumran references are similarly inapplicable. Some time after Christianity had taken hold, Hasidic Judaism did develop a narrative of a suffering messiah, but it did not exist before. In the time of Jesus, a crucified messiah would have been an oxymoron in Jewish thought. That is indeed why Paul called "Christ crucified" a "stumbling block to Jews" (1 Cor 1:23). Peter's rebuke to Jesus for suggesting the possibility typifies the common reaction.

Luke, however, seems to have been fixated on the idea that what was "fulfilled" must have been *predicted*. He assumes that if Jesus "fulfilled the Scriptures," there must have been scriptural prophecies that foretold his passion and death. In Acts 8:30-35, he indicates that Isaiah's Suffering Servant Songs were among those prophecies. But Jews have never thought of the Suffering Servant passages as messianic. They consider them to be describing Israel's mission among the nations to spread the worship of the one God. The general mission of Israel, like that of its individual prophets, is seen as constantly misunderstood, persecuted, and condemned before being vindicated by God. Jesus' story does indeed fit that narrative, but it is not the same narrative as that of Israel's Messiah.[5]

Luke, the only Gentile among the evangelists, probably did not think that he was changing the tradition. Accepting the good news that Jesus had fulfilled the Jewish Scriptures, and linking "fulfillment" to prophecy, he dramatized what he thought that meant. It is significant that when he recounts the incident of Peter's proclamation that Jesus is "the Messiah of God" (9:20), he omits Jesus' rebuke of Peter for being "human-minded" (Mark 8:33b) in not being able to reconcile messiahship with suffering. Mark and Matthew realize that Peter would have had difficulty accepting Jesus' death in the context of his mission; Luke does not.

Modern Christians, inheritors of the Gentile church, tend to accept Luke's view as normative and to think that the dividing point between early Christians and Jews was the acceptance of Jesus as the Messiah. But a close look at the Jewish understanding of the time reveals that Luke's view was the odd one; within Judaism, there were many messiahs, and all of them were defined by their successful work for God's glory. In calling Jesus "messiah," the first followers of Jesus had to redefine the meaning of the term; they had to hold it up as irony and paradox.

5. See Jon Levenson, *The Death and Resurrection of the Beloved Son* (New Haven, CT: Yale University Press, 1993). The book presents a compelling argument that "death and resurrection" is "paradigmatic to the story of Israel." It does not suggest that it is the projected narrative of a Jewish messiah.

Luke's Use of Wisdom Rhetoric

In Mark and Matthew, paradox is the language of Wisdom. Luke dramatizes the joy of unexpected outcomes—the Prodigal Son comes home, the Lost Coin is found, the Lost Sheep is carried back—but these reversals of fortune are sequential, not opposites held in tension. The closest Luke comes to paradox is when he tells how true love of neighbor is shown, not by priest or Levite, but by a "*Good* Samaritan." The Samaritans had broken away from mainstream Judaism, so to the Jews of Jerusalem, putting those two words together would have seemed absurd. Luke, however, is less interested in paradox here than in showing, one more time, that God's grace extends beyond the borders of Israel.

Luke does follow Matthew in setting up the framework of "the two ways" that pervade the Wisdom writings. In fact, he develops this perspective even further than did Matthew. When he comes to giving Jesus' list of Beatitudes, for example, he balances it with a list of "woes" (6:24-26). He makes a clear-cut division between good and evil persons: "No good tree bears bad fruit, nor again does a bad tree bear good fruit. . . . The good person . . . produces good, and the evil person . . . produces evil" (6:43-45). He uses this contrast as a prelude to the contrast between building on solid or shaky foundations (6:46-49). He shows Jesus adding a personal note to the proverb about divided kingdoms: "Whoever is not with me is against me, and whoever does not gather with me scatters" (11:23). (Notably, this saying is directly opposite to what Jesus says in Mark 9:40.)

In chapter 12, the choices get starker: "I tell you, everyone who acknowledges me before others, the [s]on of [m]an also will acknowledge before the angels of God; but whoever denies me before others will be denied before the angels of God" (12:8-9).

Next, Jesus tells a parable of the rich man who wants to build bigger barns to store all his grains for years to come; God says to him, "You fool! This very night your life is being demanded of you" (12:20). In Luke, Jesus sets the rich man's attitude in contrast to those who trust God for all things: "Therefore I tell you, do not worry about your life, what you will eat, or about your body, what you will wear. . . . If God so clothes the grass of the field, which is alive today and tomorrow is thrown into the oven, how much more will he clothe you—you of little faith!" (12:22-28).

This instruction in faith is followed by a contrast between faithful and unfaithful servants (12:41-46). Finally, Jesus announces that he himself will be a cause of division: "Do you think that I have come to bring peace to the earth? No, I tell you, but rather division" (12:51).

In chapter 13, Luke presents his own version of the Last Judgment as a "narrow gate" (13:24) and a locked door:

> When once the owner of the house has got up and shut the door, and you begin to stand outside and to knock at the door, saying, "Lord, open to us," then in reply he will say to you, "I do not know where you come from." Then you will begin to say, "We ate and drank with you, and you taught in our streets." But he will say, "I do not know where you come from; go away from me, all you evildoers!" (13:25-27)

There is some semblance here to Matthew's Last Judgment scene, but it is notably harsher: the division here is not between those who do and do not discern God's presence in their neighbor but between those who do good and those who do evil.

In Luke's version of the parable of the final wedding banquet of the kingdom, the master of the house is "enraged" by the guests who send excuses for not coming, and after ordering his servant to fill his house with others from "the roads and lanes," excludes them from his company forever: "For I tell you, none of those who were invited will taste my dinner" (14:23-24).

In Mark and Matthew, Jesus says those who seek their lives will lose them, but Luke interprets those terms to mean hating what is dear: "Whoever comes to me and does not hate father and mother, wife and children, brothers and sisters, yes, and even life itself, cannot be my disciple" (14:26). In Mark and Matthew, Jesus says one who would be "perfect" should sell all his possessions, but in Luke, that renunciation is the basic cost of discipleship: "None of you can become my disciple if you do not give up all your possessions" (14:33).

The harshness of these judgments is softened by the parables of chapter 15—the Lost Sheep, the Lost Coin, and the Lost Son— where what is lost is found. In chapter 16, however, Luke returns to stark contrasts. After telling the parable of the Dishonest Steward, Jesus concludes, "No slave can serve two masters; for a slave will either hate the one and love the other, or be devoted to the one and despise the other. You cannot serve God and wealth" (16:13). In the parable of the Rich Man and Lazarus, the Lukan Jesus projects an unbridgeable divide: "Between you and us a great chasm has been fixed, so that those who might want to pass from here to you cannot do so, and no one can cross from there to us" (16:26).

Luke's story of the persistent widow who wears down the harsh judge (18:1-8), together with the redeeming prayer of the humble tax collector (18:9-14) and the surprising salvation of Zacchaeus (19:1-10), all mitigate the image of this "chasm." At the same time, Luke himself makes no attempt to reconcile the teachings of "two ways" with the teaching of God's mercy. He simply presents them. His final dramatization of "the two ways" appears in his projection of two criminals hanging on crosses on either side of Jesus, one mocking Jesus and the other asking him to "remember" him when he comes into his kingdom (23:39-43).

Luke's Emphasis on the Holy Spirit

For Luke, Wisdom personified takes the form of "the Holy Spirit." Through the role of the Spirit, Luke expresses the divine dimension of reality. He was undoubtedly aware that God's Spirit and God's Wisdom are synonyms in the Old Testament. He may also have been mindful of the passage in the Wisdom of Solomon where Wisdom "passes into holy souls and makes them friends of God and prophets" (Wis 7:27b). Whatever the influences, he speaks of "the Spirit" as the divine force that animates Jesus and directs his narrative.

Zechariah is told that, "even before his birth," his son John "will be filled with the Holy Spirit" (1:15); Mary is told that she will conceive because "the Holy Spirit will come upon you" (1:35). Elizabeth greets Mary "filled with the Holy Spirit" (1:41), and Zechariah is "filled with the Holy Spirit" when he praises God for the gift of his son (1:67). When Simeon goes to the temple at the time of Jesus' circumcision, Luke says, "the Holy Spirit was upon him" (2:25), and further, "It had been revealed to him by the Holy Spirit that he would not see death before he had seen the Lord's Messiah" (2:26).

Luke then easily incorporates the words of John the Baptist that are also in Mark and Matthew: "He [Jesus] will baptize you with the Holy Spirit and fire" (Luke 3:16; Mark 1:8; Matt 3:11). He also repeats their image of the Spirit descending on Jesus when he himself is baptized (Luke 3:22; Mark 1:10; Matt 3:16).

Mark says that the Spirit "drove" Jesus into the wilderness (Mark 1:12), and Matthew, that "Jesus was led up by the Spirit into the wilderness" (Matt 4:1), but Luke says that "Jesus, full of the Holy Spirit . . . was led by the Spirit into the wilderness" (4:1). Luke's language implies, more than the other two, that the Spirit is guiding Jesus with God's Wisdom. In both Mark and Matthew, Jesus' ministry in Galilee begins abruptly with the arrest of John, but Luke says Jesus returned to Galilee "filled with the power of the Spirit" (4:14).

Significantly, the Lukan Jesus identifies himself with the passage from Isaiah that begins, "The Spirit of the Lord is upon me" (4:18). There is no parallel in any other gospel. Luke may have picked it because he thought it was messianic but also, one would guess, because it emphasized Jesus' relationship to God's Spirit/Wisdom.

When the Lukan Jesus teaches his disciples about prayer, he speaks of "the Holy Spirit" as God's response: "If you then, who are evil, know how to give good gifts to your children, how much more will the heavenly Father give the Holy Spirit to those who ask him!" (11:13). Matthew's account of the same episode has Jesus saying, "[H]ow much more will your Father in heaven give *good things* to those who ask him" (Matt 7:11). Luke's substitution of "Holy Spirit" for "good things" is in keeping with his general emphasis on God's Spirit (Wisdom) as the divine presence in human life.

This meaning of "the Spirit" is made clear in two other sayings that the Lukan Jesus adapts from Mark and Matthew. First, he repeats Jesus' saying about the unforgiveable sin against the Spirit in a way that makes it seem matter of fact and uncomplicated: "Everyone who speaks a word against the son of man will be forgiven; but whoever blasphemes against the Holy Spirit will not be forgiven" (Luke 12:10; Mark 3:28-29; Matt 12:31-32). Mark and Matthew both make it sound as though there is one special sin that is different from and worse than all others; Luke turns the complex saying into a simple contrast between sinning against human beings and sinning against God.

Luke then brackets this observation with one that indicates how the Spirit imparts wisdom: "When they bring you before the synagogues, the rulers, and the authorities, do not worry about how you are to defend yourselves or what you are to say; for the Holy Spirit will teach you at that very hour what you ought to say" (12:11-12). In Mark and Matthew, this advice is part of Jesus' prediction of coming tribulations his disciples will experience (Mark 13:11; Matt 10:19-20). Luke also repeats that prediction later in his gospel, but when he does, he significantly uses "wisdom" instead of "Spirit": "Make up your minds not to prepare your defense in advance; for I will give you words and a wisdom that none of your opponents will be able to withstand or contradict" (21:14-15).

Finally, in Luke's account of Jesus' crucifixion, Luke places these words from Psalm 31:6 on Jesus' dying lips: "Father, into your hands I commend my spirit" (Luke 23:46). This is a sharp departure from Mark and Matthew, who both show Jesus quoting verse one of Psalm 22: "My God, my God, why have you abandoned me?" (Mark 15:34; Matt 27:46). Both Psalm 22 and Psalm 31 start in anguish but end in joy and praise of God, so both serve the purpose of adumbrating the pattern of death and resurrection. Why, then, might Luke have found Psalm 31 the more pertinent allusion? Perhaps Luke chose the verse because of its reference to Jesus' "spirit"—which, in his mind, was the Holy Spirit of God's Wisdom. He has spoken of Jesus being conceived by the Holy Spirit; he has shown him receiving the Holy Spirit in his baptism; he has shown him acting in response to the guidance of the Spirit and advising his followers to do the same; so now he finds it fitting to show him yielding up that Spirit to God in death.

In the Acts of the Apostles, composed in the different genre of the Greek romance, the Spirit appears as a key character in the story: empowering the apostles at Pentecost (2:4), sending Philip to catechize the Ethiopian eunuch and "snatching" him back again (8:29, 39), instructing Paul as to what decision to make about circumcision for the Gentiles (15:29).

In Luke, Wisdom is personified as God's Spirit—filling Jesus from the moment he is conceived and passing on to his disciples after his death. In one sense, Luke's gospel unfolds logically, according to the principle of cause and effect. Yet at the same time, Luke points to a divine energy—God's Holy Spirit—directing the narrative in surprising ways.

God's Energy as Spirit in Luke and Teilhard

For Teilhard, too, God's energy is Spirit. It is this divine energy that is at the core of the earth and rises out of it in the form of consciousness. In fact, it is this evolving consciousness that Teilhard sees bringing about life in human form and that he perceives as still evolving. He says, "For me, Matter was the matrix of

Consciousness; and wherever we looked, Consciousness, born of Matter, was always advancing towards some Ultra-Human." He goes on to add the words quoted at the head of this chapter: "In other words, a *second species of Spirit* was emerging—and this second species was no longer directly above our heads—it lay transversely, appearing, we might say, on the horizon . . . a new sort of God of the Ahead." In Luke there is a similar perception of God always ahead of humanity, drawing it forth to divine or "ultra-human" ways. This perception is embodied in his narrative structure, in which the Spirit repeatedly calls human beings forward—first of all, Zechariah, Mary, the shepherds, and Simeon; then Jesus setting his face towards Jerusalem; and last, the disciples, called to wait, like Mary, for "the power from on high" (1:35; 24:49), who will create a new future for them.

7

John
God's Wisdom Made Flesh and Dwelling Among Us

> "I believe that the universe is an evolution.
> I believe that evolution proceeds towards spirit.
> I believe that in humankind,
> spirit is fully realized in person.[1]
> I believe that the supremely personal is the
> universal Christ."[2]

The Gospels of Mark and Matthew and Luke each has a different way of portraying the mystical dimension of Christ's story. Each succeeding gospel seems to go further in suggesting the divine aura surrounding the events. Mark embeds his story in mystery. What is riddling in Mark is clarified and linked to Scripture in Matthew. In Luke, Christ's narrative is shown to be propelled by God's Spirit. John, writing last, uses many different techniques to infuse his narrative with mystical

1. This line represents a corrected version of an earlier one (1934), added by Teilhard in 1950 in *The Heart of Matter*.

2. *Christianity and Evolution* (New York: Harcourt Brace Jovanovich, 1971), 96.

119

reality. He draws on the Jewish Wisdom traditions. He writes like a poet, often making the words and rhythms of his sentences create a subliminal experience of the event he is trying to describe. He retells the narratives of Mark, Matthew, and Luke in a way that points to their inner truth. The earlier gospels give us a bifocal lens of outer events and inner meanings. John concentrates on the second and turns the inside out.

John draws on the Wisdom traditions. From his opening word, John presents Christ as the Wisdom of God. Like Wisdom in Proverbs 8, Christ is preexistent, "in the beginning" with God (John 1:2). Like Proverbs' Wisdom, Christ is cocreator with God: "All things came into being through him" (John 1:3). Like Wisdom in Ecclesiastes 2:13 and Wisdom 7:26, Christ is light (John 1:4b-5). Like Wisdom in Sirach 15:7 and Enoch 13:2, Christ is rejected by human beings (John 1:10-11).

In his Prologue, John arranges words and rhythms so that meaning gradually unfolds in the reader's mind:

> In the beginning was the Word,
> and the Word was with God,
> and the Word was God.

Each phrase builds on the previous one and leads us deeper into the meaning of "the Word." And then John starts, as it were, all over again, going back to "the beginning" so he can go forward:

> He was in the beginning with God.
> All things came into being through him,
> and without him not one thing came into being.

Then "being" merges into "life" and "life" into "light":

> What has come into being in him was life
> and the life was the light of all people.
> The light shines in the darkness,
> and the darkness did not overcome it.

The words in themselves mimic the slow, evolutionary process of the first creation, the movement from inchoate mass to light that overcomes darkness.

Then abruptly and somewhat parenthetically, John speaks of a human witness to this light (vv. 6-8). Here the word "light" repeats, intertwines, and expands in meaning until it returns to the Word (v. 9):

> He came as a witness to testify to the light. . . .
> He himself was not the light,
> but came to testify to the light.
> The true light, which enlightens everyone,
> was coming into the world.

The words move as from primeval light into the human world. With surprising suddenness, the next verse then personifies "the light" and it takes on human contours:

> He was in the world,
> and the world came into being through him;
> yet the world did not know him.
> He came to what was his own,
> and his own people did not accept him.

Even before John proclaims, "the Word became flesh," he has dramatized it. What he says here was said before about Proverbs' Wisdom, but here it bears the impact of a living person—not just of allegorical Wisdom, but of a particular human being. Or perhaps more accurately, we understand both at the same time.

John then runs ahead of his story by saying, "But to all who received him, who believed in his name, he gave power to become children of God" (v. 12). This is more than saying, "All things came into being through him"; it is suggesting a second, spiritual creation, parallel to the first:

> who were born, not of blood
> or of the will of the flesh
> or of the will of man,
> but of God. (v. 13)

The passage adumbrates Jesus' conversation with Nicodemus that one must be "born from above" (3:3). It is only when he has brought us to this glimpse of a second creation that John articulates the heart and full dimensions of his gospel:

> And the Word became flesh
> and pitched his tent with us,
> and we have seen his glory,
> the glory as of the Father's only one [beloved],
> full of grace and truth. (v. 14)[3]

Here, John also introduces two new words he will repeat: "grace" (*charitos*) and "truth" (*aletheios*). Grace is something unearned, something given purely out of love; truth carries the implication of something verified. Together they expand on the implications of the "glory" or radiant light: it is the shining out of one who knows herself to be "beloved"; it verifies that love.

In the next two verses John expands on what this means for "the world":

---

3. The translations here of John 1:14, 16-18 are my own. They are closer to the original, literal meanings, and they are intended to convey the emphases I find in the text. For example, in v. 14, "pitched his tent" is a literal translation, and also seems to me much more vibrant than just "lived." The word "son" does not appear; John speaks of the father's "only begotten." In v. 17 the word *nomos* is conventionally translated into English as "law" but that is misleading, because we tend to identify "law" with rules and regulations; what is meant is God's *teaching*. In v. 18, the word *only begotten* reappears. Some have interpreted that in terms of the later context of the Trinity to mean that the son of God is the same as God the father; I prefer not to read in what is historically a later concept.

[Because] from his fullness
we have all received,
grace upon grace.
The teaching indeed was given through Moses;
grace and truth came through Jesus Christ. (vv.16-17)

The implication is that God's Word has always been present in the world; Christ has simply made it visible. The Word has always been present in the teaching of Moses; now we understand that teaching more clearly. We have received "grace upon grace." The grace of Moses' teaching has been verified through the grace of Christ's living. The "truth" of his living makes clear the truth of Moses' teaching. God's Word, present from the beginning, has become visible. And so John says in the final verse of his Prologue:

No one has ever seen God.
God's only begotten,
who is close to the Father's heart,
has made him known. (v. 18)

Here, the full implications of the opening verses are finally drawn out. We now understand that when John says the Word was "with" God, what he has in mind is the Word as God's "beloved"—the one who was and is in God's very bosom, God's heart. When he says, "and the Word was God," he is thinking of how one who is filled with God's love verifies that love; the beloved one makes God's love real to the world. It is both that visibility—the revelation of the divine in human flesh, and that possibility—that human beings are capable of imaging God, which John celebrates.

Throughout his gospel, John sets up Socratic dialogues between Christ and the other figures in the narrative. Because he speaks as God's Word, Christ always speaks on a level that none of his listeners can grasp. "Where did you get to know me?" Nathanael asks in chapter 1 (1:48a) and Jesus answers mysteriously, "I saw you under the fig tree before Philip called you" (1:48b). The fig tree in biblical tradition represents the tree in the Garden that, once cursed because of human sin (Gen 3:17-18), will be restored by God in the end time. So Christ's response here suggests that his knowledge extends back to the very beginning of Creation and forward to the final destiny of humanity.

In chapter 2, when Jesus drives the money changers out of the temple, some ask, "What sign can you show us for doing this?" And Jesus replies, "Destroy this temple, and in three days I will raise it up." His listeners object, "This temple has been under construction for forty-six years, and you will raise it up in three days?" (2:18-20). "But," John observes, "he was speaking of the temple of his body" (2:21). John makes it clear that Jesus speaks on a symbolic level while his accusers hear his words on a literal level and so misunderstand them. This gap between symbolic meaning and literal comprehension is a strategy John uses again and again.

In chapter 3, John presents a dialogue between Jesus and "a Pharisee named Nicodemus, a leader of the Jews." Unlike comparable dialogues in the other gospels, the conversation is not about specific rules but about the central and overriding issue of how human beings can connect with God. Nicodemus respects Jesus because of his "signs" or miracles, for, he says, "no one can do these signs that you do apart from the presence of God" (3:2). Jesus' response is not direct but on a different level than the question: "Very truly, I tell you, no one can see the kingdom of God without being born from above" (3:3). But Nicodemus misses the point because he is literal-minded: "How can anyone be born after having grown old? Can one enter a second time into the mother's womb and be born?" (3:4).

This brief exchange symbolizes the problem human beings have in understanding God's Word. Yet, as in the Socratic dialogues, the obtuseness of Nicodemus gives Christ space to expound the divine point of view more fully. First, he elaborates on what he means by being "born again":

> No one can enter the kingdom of God without being born of water and Spirit. What is born of the flesh is flesh, and what is born of the Spirit is spirit. Do not be astonished. . . .

The wind blows where it chooses, and you hear the sound of
it, but you do not know where it comes from or where it goes.
So it is with everyone who is born of the Spirit." (3:5-8)

In chapter 4, when Christ speaks on a symbolic level to a Samaritan woman, the confusion of levels is comic. After asking the
woman for a drink of water, Jesus says to her, "If you knew . . .
who it is that is saying to you, 'Give me a drink,' you would have
asked him, and he would have given you living water" (4:10). The
woman is indignant: "Sir, you have no bucket, and the well is deep.
Where do you get that living water?" (4:11). Jesus' response does
not try to clarify the riddle of his words but deepens it: "Everyone
who drinks of this water will be thirsty again, but those who drink
of the water that I will give them will never be thirsty. The water
that I will give will become in them a spring of water gushing up
to eternal life" (4:13-14). The woman stays firmly on the literal
level: "Sir, give me this water, so that I may never be thirsty or
have to keep coming here to draw water" (4:15).

When Jesus' disciples return, he has a similar exchange with
them. They urge Jesus to eat and he replies, "I have food to eat
that you do not know about" (4:32). Whereupon the disciples, as
dimwitted as Nicodemus and the Samaritan woman, say to one
another, "Surely no one has brought him something to eat?" (4:33).
In these opening episodes *everyone* Jesus speaks to—whether Jewish scholar or adulterous woman or even disciple—is equally un-
able to grasp his meaning.

The clash of symbolic and literal meaning reaches a climax in
chapter 6 when Jesus repeatedly asserts, "I am the bread of life"
(6:34, 51). It is his most profoundly mystical speech; it is received
at the most crudely literal level.

Jesus speaks of mystery: "I am the living bread that came down
from heaven. Whoever eats of this bread will live forever; and the
bread that I will give for the life of the world is my flesh" (John
6:51). His listeners respond on a mundane level: "The Jews then
disputed among themselves, saying, 'How can this man give us

his flesh to eat?'" (6:52). Therefore Jesus told them, "Those who eat my flesh and drink my blood have eternal life, and I will raise them up on the last day" (6:54).

Speaking as an ordinary human being, Jesus' discourse would make no sense, and the complaint of those listening would represent a normal reaction. But Christ is not speaking as an ordinary person and his words are steeped in symbolic, biblical references. "Bread" as the symbol for God's "Word," begins with Deuteronomy 8:3: "One does not live by bread alone, but by every word that comes from the mouth of the LORD." The idea of God's Word as bread that nourishes humanity is linked in the Old Testament to the manna God sent down to feed the people in the wilderness (Exod 16:4, 15). Psalm 78 picks up this image: "He rained on them manna to eat, and gave them the grain [bread] of heaven" (v. 24). The Wisdom of Solomon repeats it: "[Y]ou gave your people food of angels, and without their toil you supplied them from heaven with bread ready to eat" (Wis 16:20).

All of these passages underlie Jesus' "bread of life" discourse in John 6. The chapter begins with Jesus repeating the miracle of the manna by multiplying five barley loaves to feed five thousand people (John 6:1-13). When the crowd looks for Jesus the next day, he chides them for "work[ing] for the food that perishes" instead of "for the food that endures for eternal life" (John 6:27), which he subsequently identifies as "that which comes down from heaven and gives life to the world" (John 6:33). He continues: "I am the bread of life. Whoever comes to me will never be hungry" (John 6:35). The "bread that endures" is like the bread that was supplied "without their toil" in the Wisdom of Solomon; the "bread from heaven" is the manna, which, in turn, is a symbol of God's Wisdom. When Jesus says, "I am the bread of life," and "I came down from heaven" (John 6:35-38), he is identifying himself as God's Wisdom.

Reading Christ as Wisdom in the Gospel of John alters and enriches our grasp of everything that he says. When, for example, Christ says, "I am the light of the world. Whoever follows me will never walk in darkness" (8:12), some Christians may interpret this passage as a validation of their beliefs. At the same time, others who are not Christian might see this interpretation as insufferable arrogance. Either way, both restrict the meaning of the words to their own particular knowledge. But what if this passage is read as Wisdom speaking? Then Christ's words are set free from the narrow identity of this person or that religious group whom the reader knows. The words become understood as oracular and indeterminate; they contain the mystery appropriate to divine speech.

The repeated identification of Jesus with "God the Father" reinforces the idea that Jesus' words should be heard as beyond total human comprehension. What Augustine said about knowing God is applicable here: "If you think you understand God, then that which you understand is not God."[4] John dramatizes a similar idea: if Christ is God's Word, John suggests, do not expect to grasp easily or fully who he is or what he means.

The elusive identity of the Johannine Jesus comes to a climax in his final discourse. Thomas protests, "Lord, we do not know where you are going. How can we know the way?" (14:5) and Jesus responds: "I am the way, and the truth, and the life. No one comes to the Father except through me" (14:6). Again, this passage can be read either as narrowly restrictive or broadly inclusive. If it is interpreted to mean that only those who identify themselves specifically as Christians can know God, then the saying excludes a large part of humanity. But if it is interpreted to mean that all those who pursue Wisdom can know God, then it casts a wide net, embracing all who seek to be wise.

Understanding John's gospel in this broader framework gives it greater depth and more universal significance. Then we can read the "I AM" speeches as ones that give expression to different aspects of Wisdom. "I am," the Johannine Jesus says: "the bread of life" (6:35, 41, 48), the "light of the world" (8:12; 12:46), "the gate" (10:3) and "the good shepherd" (10:11), "the resurrection" (11:25),

---

4. Sermon 2.16 on Matthew 3:13.

and "the true vine" (15:1). We have just looked at the tradition of God's Word as bread. Wisdom as light has a similar tradition. The psalmist says, "Your word is a lamp to my feet and a light to my path" (Ps 119:105), and in the Wisdom of Solomon, Wisdom is described as "a reflection of eternal light" (7:26), "more beautiful than the sun" (7:29a), and, in fact, "compared with the light she is found to be superior" (7:29b). Wisdom as a gate follows from the image of Wisdom as a "way" or "path." Wisdom as a shepherd appears at the end of Psalm 119—that great paean to the law or teaching of God—when the psalmist laments, "I have gone astray like a lost sheep" (Ps 119:176), and begs God to seek him out; the implication is that God's teaching (Word/Wisdom) is like a shepherd that will bring the psalmist home.

Wisdom as "the resurrection and the life" (John 11:25) is a concept expressed several times in the Wisdom of Solomon. At the close of the narrative about the wicked plotting the death of "the righteous one," the author interjects:

> Thus they reasoned, but they were led astray,
> for their wickedness blinded them,
> and they did not know the secret purposes of God,
> nor hoped for the wages of holiness,
> nor discerned the prize for blameless souls;
> for God created us for incorruption,
> and made us in the image of his own eternity. (Wis 2:21-23)

Later in the work, when Solomon speaks of pursuing Wisdom, he says, "Because of her I shall have immortality" (Wis 8:13) and "in kinship with wisdom there is immortality" (Wis 8:17). These passages are themselves an echo and development of Wisdom's own speech in Proverbs: "Whoever finds me finds life . . . all who hate me love death" (Prov 8:35-36).

Jesus/Wisdom as "the true vine" (John 15:1) is the last of the symbolic comparisons in John. The most obvious meaning of the analogy is that a vine is the life-giving source for the fruit that hangs from it. In Old Testament imagery, "the vineyard of the

Lᴏʀᴅ of hosts is the house of Israel" (Isa 5:7). Hosea reflects, "Israel is a luxuriant vine that yields its fruit" (Hos 10:1). In Jeremiah, God complains about Israel, "I planted you as a choice vine. . . . How then did you . . . become a wild vine?" (Jer 2:21). Psalm 80 uses similar imagery, with the psalmist pleading for new life for the vine:

> Turn again, O God of hosts;
>   look down from heaven, and see;
> have regard for this vine,
>   the stock that your right hand planted. (vv. 14-15)

The psalm continues by identifying the vine with God's "son," specifically, "the son of man":

> and on the son you made strong for yourself . . .
> Let your hand be on the man of your right hand,
> on the son of man whom you made strong for yourself.
>   (vv. 13-18)[5]

The implicit connection between "the vine," which is Israel, and "the son of man" is an intriguing one. Both in Psalm 8 and in Ezekiel, "the son of man" is an alternate name for "human being" and emphasizes the distance between humanity and divinity. Jesus refers to himself as the son of man throughout the Synoptic Gospels and once in John, when he confronts the blind man he had cured, and asks, "Do you believe in the son of man?" (John 9:35). Scholars argue over whether "son of man" in the gospels should be understood as an apocalyptic title or as a way of speaking about common humanity. More than anything else, the arguments reflect one's larger understanding of who or what Jesus represents. In John, Jesus mostly refers to himself as "son of God," a way of speaking appropriate to

5. A literal translation, not found in the NRSV or JSB, but given by Raymond Brown in his commentary on the Gospel of John (New York: Doubleday, 1970), 670.

his status as Wisdom. Yet he also represents Wisdom *made flesh*, and as such it is fitting that he also call himself son of man.

In John's view (as in Matthew's and Mark's) Jesus as "son of man" is a surrogate for Israel, the fleshly dwelling place for God's Wisdom. It is a specific dwelling, yet not one restricted to one place or people but symbolic of all who are enlightened by God's Wisdom. As such, Christ can be portrayed as "the true vine," the essential link between all humanity and divinity. Christ pleads with his disciples to "abide" in him (15:5, 6, 7, 9, 10) and "bear fruit" (15:16).

The vine imagery in John symbolizes not only the necessary connection between Jesus and his followers but also the intimate relationship between Jesus and the Father.

That insistence on unity goes further than simply "boasting that God is his Father"; it indicates a oneness of being between Jesus and God that is unique. Such unique unity fits John's portrayal of Jesus as God's Wisdom—an aspect of God's very being. It is as God's Wisdom that the Johannine Jesus can say, "If you knew me, you would know my Father also" (8:19b), and "the Father is in me and I am in the Father" (10:38), and "the word that you hear is not mine, but is from the Father who sent me" (14:24b). It is as God's Wisdom that he can say, "No one can come to me unless drawn by the Father" (6:44), or that he can respond with some exasperation to Philip, "How can you say, 'Show us the Father'? Do you not believe that I am in the Father and the Father is in me?" (14:9-10). If one grasps that Christ is speaking as God's Word, all these sayings fall into place.

John's portrayal of Jesus as God's Word also underlies the fierce exchanges between Jesus and "the Jews" who protest that "Abraham is our father" (8:39). If these dialogues are read as historical conversations between a particular human being and the Jewish people, they are unmitigated slander of the Jews. They only make sense as exchanges between God's Word and the people who were granted the gift of God's Word in the Torah. John dramatizes, in effect, what he sees as deafness on the part of his fellow Jews to Jesus as God's Word. Grasping that fact won't make the dialogue seem much better to modern Jews, but maybe it can give some nuance to its meaning for modern Christians: they should read John's words not as an indictment of Judaism but as John's plea to understand Jesus as the true representative of Judaism's teaching—the Word of God. In the context of John's time, this was still a family quarrel; over the centuries, in increasingly more and more Gentile contexts, it has come to seem like a quarrel between Christians and Jews. But Christians should know that such a reading is an anachronism—and a tragic one, at that.

For John, Jesus as "the true vine" means that Jesus is the true Torah connecting human beings with the divine. Through this image, Christ, the Word, stresses not only his intimacy with God the Father but his desired intimacy with his followers. He—God's Wisdom—seeks to bring his followers into the same kind of intimacy with God. So he says, "Those who love me will keep my word, and my Father will love them, and we will come to them and make our home with them" (14:23).

As in the Prologue, John underlines his meaning through his arrangement of words. Here, he creates a vine through the intertwining of the word "abide." Christ repeats it eleven times in six verses:

> *Abide* in me as I *abide* in you. Just as the branch cannot bear fruit unless it *abides* in the vine, neither can you unless you *abide* in me. I am the vine, you are the branches. Those who *abide* in me and I in them bear much fruit, because apart from me you can do nothing. Whoever does not *abide* in me is thrown away. . . . If you *abide* in me, and my words *abide* in you, ask for whatever you wish. . . . As the Father has loved me, so I have loved you; *abide* in my love. If you keep my commandments, you will *abide* in my love, just as I have kept the Father's commandments and *abide* in his love. (15:4-10)

The Greek root for the word "abide" or "dwell" (*mevo*) is the same word that Jesus uses at the beginning of John 14: "In my Father's house there are many dwelling places" (v. 2). In John 14,

Jesus offers this as a comforting statement to reassure his disciples because he is about to leave them. In John 15, Jesus indicates that they can *dwell/abide* in his commandments and his love. In John 14, Jesus also assures his followers that the Father will send them "another Advocate" (14:16), that is, "the Holy Spirit" who "will teach you everything" (14:26). Through this teaching they can continue to abide or dwell in God's Word, God's Wisdom.

In 2 Kings, Elisha asks Elijah for "a double share" of his spirit before he ascends into heaven (2 Kgs 2:9). In the Wisdom of Solomon, the author asks God, "Who has learned your counsel, unless you have given wisdom and sent your [H]oly [S]pirit from on high?" (Wis 9:17). And in his praise of Wisdom, the author speaks of how, "in every generation," Wisdom "passes into holy souls and makes them friends of God, and prophets" (Wis 7:27). He continues, "[F]or God loves nothing so much as the person who lives [*dwells*] with Wisdom" (Wis 7:28). In the Hebrew Bible, God's Holy Spirit is equated with God's Wisdom. So the human being who dwells with Wisdom dwells with God. In John 20, Christ specifically "breathes" on his disciples and says, "Receive the Holy Spirit" (20:22). Like Elijah, Christ leaves his disciples a portion of his Spirit—that is, his Wisdom. As in the Wisdom of Solomon, Jesus arranges for Wisdom to "pass into holy souls and make them friends of God, and prophets."

John's focus on the mystical significance of Christ's story becomes the most vivid if one compares the episodes in the Synoptics to John's rendering of the same events.

Each gospel opens differently. In Mark, the first word is simply "Beginning" (*archē*) without an article before it, triggering, in Jewish biblical memory, the opening of Genesis and the self-description of Proverbs' Wisdom as the "beginning" of Creation (Prov 8:22). Matthew's beginning, on the other hand, recalls "the book of the generations" at the start of Genesis 2. Luke resets the narrative in a seemingly historical context. John cuts right to the spiritual core: "In the beginning was the Word . . . and the Word was God."

Each gospel moves quickly to John the Baptist as the forerunner of Christ. Mark and Matthew use almost identical words to describe John's appearance in the Judean desert, looking like Elijah. Luke omits this comparison and portrays John as simply one who prophesies Christ's coming. John omits all the descriptive details and speaks of John as "witness to the light."

In the Synoptics, God twice calls Jesus "my beloved Son"—first at his baptism, and then again at his transfiguration. John greatly expands this suggestion of Christ's intimacy with the Father: first in his Prologue, where he describes Jesus as the Father's "beloved," and more than once in Christ's speech, where Christ proclaims, in various ways, "the Father and I are one."

The Synoptic Gospels first describe baptism as a ritual of repentance administered by John and later as a rite of initiation into fellowship with Christ. Only John, however, speaks of baptism as the foundational condition of spiritual life: "you must be born from above" (John 3:7).

In the Synoptics, Christ seeks out his followers. In John, however, disciples seek out Christ, asking him where he lives. Christ's response is inviting but mysterious: "Come and see" (John 1:39).

The first part of each Synoptic Gospel is filled with Christ's miracles: the blind see, the mute speak, and the lame walk. Many lives—especially those of women—are transformed by Christ's touch: Peter's mother-in-law is cured of a fever; a woman with a long-lasting hemorrhage is healed; a little girl is brought back to life. In John, however, the miracles or "signs" are of a different order. Water is changed into wine, a sign of humanity being transformed into divinity. Christ proclaims himself to be the water that quenches all thirst, as well as "the living bread come down from heaven." A man three days dead walks out of his tomb, a sign, Christ says explicitly, that he, Christ, is himself "the resurrection and the life." In John, it is not what Christ does, but who Christ is, that is the miracle.

In the Synoptics, Christ gives many different instructions, all aspects of his maxim that the one who would gain life must first lose it. In John, there is only one commandment, writ large and clear. "I give you a new commandment, that you love one another. Just as I have loved you, you also should love one another" (13:34);

"No one has greater love than this, to lay down one's life for one's friends" (15:13).

In Mark, Matthew, and Luke, all give the same basic narrative of Christ's last supper—one that follows the account given by Paul in 1 Corinthians 12: "On the night before he died, Jesus took bread, broke it and said, 'This is my body, that is given for you.' . . . Then he took the wine, saying, 'This is my blood . . . poured out for you. . . . Do this in remembrance of me.'" Remarkably, in John there is no such account. Jesus does celebrate a final meal with his disciples, but instead of breaking bread and pouring out wine, he ties a towel around his waist and washes his disciples' feet (13:1-15). This simple and surprising action serves to interpret the meaning of the meal he shares with his followers: "For I have set you an example, that you should also do as I have done to you" (13:15). In the other accounts, Jesus' sharing of his body and blood suggests, on the one hand, his total self-giving and, on the other, his mystical unity with those who consume these gifts of his being. In John's narrative, the focus shifts to the effect of this unity: a life given over, like Christ's, to the serving of others. The mystical aura hovers not over the bread and wine per se but over the intimacy, the self-giving communion of Christ's imitators. "The body of Christ" is revealed to be not just a single male form but a community of those who serve. In the other gospels, Jesus instructs his followers to put themselves last, saying, "Behold I am among you as one who serves." Here in John, he dramatizes that saying and makes explicit its implications. Christ's action here anticipates what will be spelled out later in the commandment to "love one another as I have loved you" (15:12). It anticipates and interprets the meaning of the cross: "No one has greater love than this, to lay down one's life for one's friends" (15:13). Through Jesus' foot-washing gesture, John shows that the laying down of one's life is not just a single act but an ongoing habit of service.

The resurrection of Christ is also treated differently in John than in the other gospels. First of all, there is no transfiguration scene that reveals Christ's divinity or anticipates his glory after death. On the contrary, John presents Christ as glorified from the beginning. When Jesus speaks of his coming death to Nicodemus, he describes it as being "lifted up" (3:14). By this means, John suggests that being "lifted up" on the cross is the same as being lifted up to new life. Even at the moment of being sentenced to death, the Johannine Jesus says, "I lay down my life. No one takes it from me" (10:18). He chooses his death as he chooses his life. At the moment of death, he does not cry out to the Father as he does in the Gospels of Mark, Matthew, and Luke. Instead, he says, as one who has accomplished his mission, "It is finished" (John 19:30). In spite of his suffering, Christ never appears weak or vulnerable in John. His divine self is present throughout.

Yet John does suggest that there is a shift in Christ's body and bodily appearance after death. Mary Magdalene does not recognize him right away, and he cautions her not to "hold on" to him because he has "not yet ascended" to the Father (20:17). So John indicates that although Christ is always one with the Father, there are stages in the process by which his body becomes Spirit.

Most striking of all is the way John projects the future of Christ's disciples. In both Mark and Matthew, Jesus promises his followers that he will be "going ahead" of them to Galilee. There is a sense in both these gospels of Christ's ministry recycling through his disciples. In Luke, the idea of Christ's disciples carrying on his work is made explicit in Christ's final promise of the Spirit. In John, Jesus passes on both his Spirit and his "peace." He makes it clear that it is not the world's peace he is bestowing but God's fullness that "surpasses all understanding." In Mark and Matthew, the future is obscure and uncertain. In Luke, Jesus sends his disciples into danger, "like lambs among wolves." The continuing hardships and perils of their lives is further illustrated in the Acts of the Apostles. But in John, Christ promises his followers that they will do what he has done, and even "greater works than these" (14:12). What did he mean?

Evolving Humanity in John and in Teilhard

As in the other gospels, Christ speaks of his return to his disciples, but in a different way. In Mark and Matthew, he promises a return to the Galilean ministry. In Luke, he promises to send the Spirit to empower his disciples in new ways. In John, he says he "will not leave you orphaned" (14:18). He says that if they keep his word, he and the Father will come to them and "dwell" with them. He also says that if he does not go away, the Spirit cannot come to them, and the Spirit will "teach [them] everything" (14:26). In John, as in no other gospel, there is a sense of Christ as a divine yet transitional figure, preparing the way for human beings to follow. "As the Father has sent me," he says, "so I send you" (20:21) He seems to be talking to all his disciples collectively, present and future. He must go away so that they—collectively— can come together in the Spirit and do what he has done and "even greater works than these." If they do, they will achieve that peace which is beyond the world's imagining. Collectively, they will be the second coming of Christ.

John, of course, does not speak of "evolution"; the word would not have been in his vocabulary. But from the Prologue to the final discourses of Christ, John indicates his belief in a dynamic, evolving presence of divine being in the world. The Prologue poetically dramatizes the gradual emergence of God's "Word" into a person. In Christ's farewell discourses to his disciples, John shows Christ speaking of a future in which Christ himself will disappear from view and the Spirit will take over, teaching new things and empowering Christ's followers to do what he had done "and even greater things than these." Implicitly, John and Teilhard share the same view of matter evolving into person, and persons evolving, collectively, into Spirit.

8

"The Flesh Made Word"
Humanity Evolving
Towards a Unifying Consciousness?

John had a mystical vision of the future disciples of Christ as collectively forming Christ's second coming into the world. It is a vision similar to that of Teilhard de Chardin. John's vision was rooted in the science and literary expression of an ancient world. Teilhard's vision speaks the language of our own time. I invite the reader to review with me salient aspects of Teilhard's vision of human evolution and then, with that as a framework, to revisit the biblical wisdom of this book.

The Vision of Teilhard

Teilhard saw human evolution as a slow process of growth in consciousness. The kind of gradual expansion of awareness that every person undergoes, to one extent or another, in the course of a normal lifetime, Teilhard saw writ large in the gradual maturing of humanity over centuries of time. Since this growth takes place over millions or billions of years, its pace is too infinitesimal for any single human generation to notice; Teilhard projected it on the dual basis of his scientific understanding of evolution in general and his religious understanding of the human vocation to grow in the Spirit. He uses both the language of Science and the language of Religion to express his vision, yet wanting to get away from—or beyond—the conventional understandings of either field, he also coined words and invented unusual phrases. He speaks, for example, of the human being moving towards the "Ultra-Human" as a way to suggest human beings stretching—not beyond their real limits, but beyond their conventional expectations. Or he speaks of God "incorporating" the human being, and the human being "completing" God, in order to express his view that, when the divine and the human merge, the result is mutual transformation. He saw that the meaning of "God" is transformed by the human perception of God's caring involvement in human experience. He believed human beings may be said to "complete" God to the extent that they reflect God—that is, to the extent of their "divinization."

Teilhard elevated the feminine aspect of the divine because he perceived "the eternal feminine" as the "unitive" element in the universe—that is, as the disposition to attract, and be attracted to, the Other. In that relationship of mutual attraction he found the creative energy of the universe—a creative energy scientifically evident in the realm of physics, chemistry, and biology, psychologically evident in the realm of human love, and mystically evident in the realm of divine love. He saw scientific truth as analogy for the spiritual: in each instance, attraction leading to union, and union to a new creation. With Dante, he saw Love as "the force that moves the sun and the other stars."

Moving from scientific to mystical experience, Teilhard came to see that attracting and sustaining divine Love everywhere, in every thing and every aspect of human life. Through his work he tried to raise human consciousness of this divine love, which he perceived not only as a sphere enveloping human existence ("the divine milieu") but also as a magnet, calling humanity into a divinely transformed future ("the Noosphere").[1] He saw it as a future in which human beings would collectively merge with, and reflect, that divine love, so that All would be One.

Teilhard's Vision in Biblical Wisdom

Does Scripture contain anything of Teilhard's mystical vision of human evolution? I invite the reader to revisit the sacred literature of this book and reflect with me on the different expressions of evolving humanity in the gospels, the Creed, the writings of Paul, Ascent literature, and the Jewish Wisdom writings—not least, in the wisdom of Job.

In the Gospels

In the Western church, it is conventional to focus almost exclusively on the incarnational aspects of the gospels—the way in which their narratives dramatize the Word or Wisdom of God made flesh. But in the Eastern church, it is equally important to notice the way in which they teach the reverse—that is, the call to human beings to become, individually and collectively, living embodiments of God's Word. In this perspective, the gospels are not simply contemplative, detached views of what Wisdom looks like in the person of Christ. They are also kinetic, urging their readers to become like Christ—that is, preaching how weak and vulnerable flesh can, and should, be transformed by God's Wisdom. The other side of incarnation is divinization. Or to put it another way, *the Word made flesh* implies *the flesh made Word.* This call to transformed humanity appears in each gospel in a characteristically different way.

John's Prologue states that the incarnation of the Word "gave power" to others "to become children of God" (1:12). What that

---

1. Teilhard invented the word "Noosphere" by combining the word "sphere" with the Greek word for "mind" or "intellect" (*nous*) in order to convey his thesis that the human species is designed to evolve in a spiritual, not a physical, way. See *The Phenomenon of Man*, trans. Bernard Wall (New York: Harper and Brothers, 1959), 180–84.

might look like is modeled in John's gospel by Jesus, who is constantly mindful that he is the son of God. That mindfulness does not lead to lording it over others but quite the contrary: to the washing of their feet. This action in John provides a concrete image for the instruction Jesus gives to his disciples in the other gospels to become servants to others (Mark 10:42-45; Matt 20:25-28; Luke 22:24-27). Such an act transcends the normal human instinct to control rather than to serve. John indicates such a transformation can come only thorough the receiving of the Spirit—that is, God's Wisdom (16:13; 14:26). In John, receiving God's Spirit means receiving God's peace and, with it, the power to bring peace, to forgive (14:27; 20:21-23). Serving, forgiving, and bringing peace to others are signs of human transformation. They indicate an enhanced consciousness of God's presence in human life. And in John, Jesus promises those who follow him will be able to do what he has done and even "greater works than these" (14:12).

Luke shows the Spirit as the primary agent of human change. Reception of the Spirit comes through the asking. As Jesus says in Luke: "How much more will the heavenly Father give the Holy Spirit to those who ask him!" (11:13). At the same time, reception of the Spirit involves the willingness to be changed by the Spirit. The openness to being transformed in a way beyond one's imagining, is modeled by Mary's *fiat* (1:38), "How can this be?" she asks at first. And yet responds, "Let it be with me according to your word."

In Matthew, the vision of human lives transformed by God's grace appears most vividly in the Beatitudes (5:3-12). Matthew also shows, through the parables of the Weeds (13:24-30), the Lost Sheep (18:2-14), and the Laborers in the Vineyard (20:1-16), what is involved in taking on God's view of things. Compassion for each human person transforms human attitudes: the weeds are allowed to grow; the solitary sheep is sought; the late worker in the vineyard is paid as much as those who came early. This transformed vision allows one to discern the divine presence in the hungry, the sick, and the imprisoned (Matt 25:3-46).

In Mark, the vision of human transformation is embodied in the way he describes the person of Jesus. Like God's Word in

Scripture, Jesus' identity is a secret that has to be discovered. It is revealed to three men when he is "transfigured before them" and declared to be God's "beloved" (9:2, 7). It is revealed to a Roman soldier when he sees Jesus in death (15:39). It is revealed to three women who find his tomb empty and come to understand that he has been raised (16:6). In this final moment, the ecstasy experienced throughout Mark's gospel—the ecstasy of those who witness the various miracles that transform human lives—is brought to a climax. The tomb is empty; death is no longer to be feared. The women are "possessed" by an expanded consciousness of human destiny.

Every gospel leaves that destiny in some sense unfinished, still to be fully realized in the future.

In the Creed

Christians tend to think of the gospels as the presentation of definitive facts and moral teachings; indeed, we often speak of "the Gospel message." Yet a careful hearing or reading of the gospels, as we have just seen, shows that far from presenting a closed set of facts or a finished story, the gospels invite their readers into an ongoing drama, an unfinished process. If we read the Creed in its full, original context, we will find that it does the same.

First of all, the Creed expresses belief in God making all things "visible and invisible." What is meant by the "invisible" is left undefined; the words simply imply faith in a spiritual world that is also part of the human experience. The vagueness of the designation is also openness; the human grasp of what is invisible is left open to continuing expansion.

Second, the description of Christ is largely and consciously taken, as we have seen, from the language of Wisdom in Proverbs 8. The "only begotten son of God" echoes Wisdom describing herself as one whom God "begot." The phrase, "born of the Father before all ages," recalls Wisdom saying that she was beside God at the first moment of Creation; "through him all things were made" echoes Wisdom saying she was there "as a master artisan." The Creed says that Christ "came down from heaven" for the sake of humanity, just as Wisdom says her "constant delight" was to be with human beings. What are the implications of this metaphorical comparison of Christ to Proverbs' Wisdom? It implies that, for John, Christ embodied the divine Wisdom—the alluring, life-giving, nurturing, feminine aspects of divine being.

The description of God's Son being born and coming into the world for a purpose further evokes the image of a divine being that changes or evolves. This sense of an evolving person is further developed in the description of Christ returning to heaven by rising and ascending and "com[ing] again in glory." In other words, Christ is envisioned not as a static being but as one in constant motion.

Evolving participation in divinity is also emphasized in the expression of belief in "the Holy Spirit, . . . giver of life . . . who has spoken through the prophets." Just as God's Son is characterized as God's Wisdom in human flesh, "the Holy Spirit" is characterized as one who speaks God's Wisdom through human voices.

The concluding paragraph of the Creed expresses belief in further human divinization, in spiritual evolution yet to come. First, there is assertion of belief in "one, holy, catholic, and apostolic Church." While church members would like to see these attributes as facts, realistically every believer knows he or she is expressing faith in a vision yet to be realized.

The believer next confesses "one baptism for the forgiveness of sins"—an acknowledgment of universal sinfulness and so the need for future forgiveness.

Last of all, the believer explicitly expresses faith in future divinization: "I look forward to the resurrection of the dead and the life of the world to come." Again, precisely what that means is not defined; it is left open to the future. Yet however one understands it, the assertion expresses the believer's faith that human beings will evolve still further.

In Paul

Paul's continual emphasis is on the transformation of human life—both now and in the future. First Corinthians stresses the transforming power of God's wisdom. Although Paul notes that the members of his community are not wise or powerful by human standards, he sees that in Christ, "God chose what is foolish in the world. . . . God chose what is weak in the world. . . . God chose what is low and despised in the world" (1 Cor 1:27-28) in order to show the full potential of divinized humanity.

If the members of his community align themselves with the divinized humanity represented by Christ, their lives should be transformed like his. They should not be divided: "For all things are yours, whether Paul or Apollos or Cephas or the world or life or death or the present or the future—all belong to you, and you belong to Christ, and Christ belongs to God" (1 Cor 3:21-23). They should not sin with their bodies, for "Do you not know that your bodies are members of Christ?" (1 Cor 6:15). Being members of the body of Christ is in itself divinizing, bestowing on each person a special gift of the Spirit (1 Cor 12:4-27). Above all, it bestows the capacity to love as God loves—bearing, believing, hoping, and enduring all things (1 Cor 13:7).

Through this kind of loving, the human person matures in sharing the divine life: "For now we see in a mirror, dimly [in a riddle], but then we will see face to face. Now I know only in part; then I will know fully, even as I have been fully known" (1 Cor 13:12). The idea of spiritual growth is a repeated theme in Paul. Earlier in 1 Corinthians he tells his community that when he first came to them, he treated them "as infants in Christ" (1 Cor 3:1), and in 1 Thessalonians, he speaks of nurturing them as gently "like a nurse tenderly caring for her own children" (1 Thess 2:7).

For Paul, the impetus for spiritual growth is the conviction that Christ was raised from the dead. Knowing that Christ was raised gives all human beings hope that death is not the end:

> If Christ has not been raised, your faith is futile and you are still in your sins. . . . If for this life only we have hoped in Christ, we are of all people most to be pitied.

> But in fact Christ has been raised from the dead, the first
> fruits of those who have died. For since death came through
> a human being, the resurrection of the dead has also come
> through a human being; for as all die in Adam, so all will be
> made alive in Christ. (1 Cor 15:17-22)

Paul's reference to Christ as the "first fruits" implies his belief that Christ's resurrection is not to be considered unique but rather the first of many such events. As he says in Romans, Christ is "the firstborn within a large family" (Rom 8:29). For Paul, Christ's resurrection is a model for the whole human race. Using the analogy of seed buried in earth and then rising to a new and transformed life, he says:

> So it is with the resurrection of the dead. What is sown is
> perishable, what is raised is imperishable. . . . It is sown a
> physical body, it is raised a spiritual body. Thus it is written,
> "The first man, Adam, became a living being"; the last Adam
> became a life-giving spirit. . . . Just as we have borne the
> image of the man of dust, we will also bear the image of the
> man of heaven. (1 Cor 15:42-49)

What precisely is meant by a "spiritual body" is mysterious and mystical. All that is clear is that Paul believes that human beings are destined for an existence in which they will be embodied and yet divinely transformed.

Here in 1 Corinthians he seems to be talking about something that will transpire at the end of time when Christ "hands over the kingdom to God the Father . . . so that God may be all in all" (1 Cor 15:24, 28). Elsewhere Paul seems to envision the possibility of a human life transformed here and now—a radical transformation that anticipates the "spiritual body" to come.

Paul appears to project both a final, ultimate transformation and an immediate, ongoing process of change. So, for example, he says, "All of us, with unveiled faces, seeing the glory of the Lord as though reflected in a mirror, are being transformed into the same image from one degree of glory to another; for this comes from the Lord, the Spirit" (2 Cor 3:1-18).

He prays that the members of his community may grow in holiness: "May the Lord make you increase and abound in love for one another and for all" (1 Thess 3:12). Or more fully:

> I am confident of this, that he who began a good work among you will bring it to completion . . . My prayer [is] that your love may overflow more and more with knowledge and full insight to help you determine what is best, so that in the day of Christ you may be pure and blameless. (Phil 1:6; 9-10)

Paul also sees transformation into holiness—that is, divinization—as a process that involves struggle and setbacks. Although he does not, of course, use the word "evolution," what he describes is a transformation of the whole earth and a parallel between the slow and difficult changing of the earth and the transformation of the human being:

> We know that the whole creation has been groaning in labor pains until now; and not only the creation, but we ourselves, who have the first fruits of the Spirit, groan inwardly while we wait for adoption, the redemption of our bodies. . . .
>
> Likewise the Spirit helps us in our weakness; for we do not know how to pray as we ought, but that very Spirit intercedes with sighs too deep for words. (Rom 8:22-23, 26)

In Ascent Literature

The literature of Ascent also has parallels to Teilhard's perspective of human destiny. In the Teilhardian context, it is worth repeating the observations made by Martha Himmelfarb:

> The claim that a human being can become the equal of angels stands at the center of early Jewish and Christian apocalypses in which ascent to heaven is the mode of revelation. . . . The apocalypses with transformation of men

into angels belong to one strand of a large body of literature that treats the biblical patriarchs and especially Moses as in some sense divine.[2]

It is also worth repeating that these writings involve the three key elements that, according to Gershom Sholem, mark Jewish mysticism: human ascent into the heavenly realm; the revelation of cosmic, heavenly secrets; and human ecstasy. It is worth reflecting as well that these writings, dating from the third century BCE to the second century CE, are both Jewish and Christian. Does this not suggest that Christian origins are particularly rooted in Jewish mysticism?

In this context it is worth repeating how these key elements of Jewish mysticism are present in the much misunderstood ending of Mark: Jesus ascends from the grave; the women who discover the empty tomb simultaneously discover the secret of human destiny; the effect on them is ecstasy (*ekstasis*). Perhaps the ending of the earliest gospel has been misunderstood because it relies so heavily on the mystical traditions that have been lost or diminished in the Western church.

In the Jewish Wisdom Writings

The Wisdom writings are usually treated as practical guides to holiness—as indeed they are. But they also express a yearning to transcend the visible limitations of human life and a belief in this possibility. All of these writings concur in perceiving that human beings can share in divine wisdom. Wisdom is the bridge between divinity and humanity. Wisdom in fact transforms the human being into a reflection of the divine. The authors of the Wisdom writings assume that there is a natural human longing for this transformation. In many instances, the Wisdom writings express this natural longing by imagining Wisdom as a beautiful woman, worthy of being pursued as a lover pursues his beloved. As "Solomon" says:

2. *Ascent to Heaven in Jewish and Christian Apocalypses* (New York: Oxford University Press, 1993), 3.

> I loved her and sought her from my youth;
> I desired to take her for my bride,
> and became enamored of her beauty. (Wis 8:2)

In this Jewish work, written a century and a half before the gospels, the relationship between the author and Wisdom is a mystical one. Wisdom is Spirit—"all-powerful, overseeing all" (Wis 7:23), "a breath of the power of God" (7:25), "a reflection of eternal light, a spotless mirror of the working of God, and an image of his goodness" (7:26). This divine Spirit "passes into holy souls and makes them friends of God, and prophets" (7:27b).

In other Wisdom writings, Wisdom is identified with the Torah, and so "the lover" in these works is one who, in the words of Psalm 1, meditates on God's law "day and night." The book of Sirach brings these two ideas most forcibly together, making explicit the connection between Wisdom and the Torah while at the same time borrowing imagery from the Song of Songs to convey the ardor of the author's longing for divine wisdom. Sirach says that he pursued Wisdom "like a hunter . . . who peers through her windows and listens at her doors; who camps near her house . . . who pitches his tent near her " (Sir 14:20-25). And Woman Wisdom says to her lover, "Come to me, you who desire me, and eat your fill of my fruits" (Sir 24:19).

The love imagery of Solomon and Sirach communicate the mystical experience of the human being in search of divine wisdom. In each case, the imagery makes it clear that the author is seeking not a dry set of rules or restrictive regulations but a transformative, joyous way of living. In the Song of Songs this mystical relationship is expressed most sensuously, and so most vividly. In fact, it is the very sensuousness of the Song that conveys the depth of the mystical experience. (One might compare Teilhard's vision of the "amorization" of the universe.)[3] It is surely this mystical

---

3. See chap. 3, n. 13.

dimension of the Song that made the rabbis refer to it as a "parable" or riddle that brings one to understand the whole Bible.

The Wisdom Psalms also depict a human way of life that delights in sharing the divine life. The wisdom seekers of Psalm 1 are "like trees planted by streams of water" whose "leaves do not wither" (v. 3). In Psalm 19, "The law of the LORD is perfect, reviving the soul" (v. 7a). This "law"—that is, Wisdom—transforms the simple into the wise (v. 7b). Because of their transforming power, God's ordinances are to be desired even more than "fine gold" (v. 10a); to the seeker of wisdom they are "sweeter also than honey, and drippings of the honeycomb" (v. 10b).

Similarly in Psalm 119, that lengthy celebration of God's law, the psalmist says, "I delight in the way of your decrees" (v. 14) and again, "I will delight in your statutes" (v. 16), and "lead me in the path of your commandments, for I delight in it" (v. 35). God's statutes, he says, have been his "songs" (v. 54). As in Psalm 19, the speaker tastes God's word and finds it delectable: "How sweet are your words to my taste, sweeter than honey to my mouth" (v. 103). As in Psalm 19, the speaker here also finds God's wisdom transformative: "The unfolding of your words gives light; it imparts understanding to the simple" (v. 130). At the very end, the psalmist speaks of himself as a "lost sheep"; by implication, God's wisdom is a shepherd bringing him home. There is a subtle link here to the narrative of transformation in Psalm 23, where the speaker starts out as a sheep and ends as an honored guest "in the house of the LORD" (Ps 23:6).

The power of God's wisdom to delight and transform are the overarching themes of the Wisdom writings. In Ecclesiastes, as we have seen, a narrative turning point occurs when the cynical Preacher observes, "Wisdom makes one's face to shine" (Eccl 8:1). In Baruch, God's wisdom is what gives life (Bar 4:1b).

Both themes are present in the initial portraits of Wisdom in Proverbs. In Proverbs 8, Wisdom is beside God at Creation, and whether we interpret that to mean Wisdom was God's companion or instrument or cocreator, it is clear that Wisdom is conceived as that aspect or dimension of the divine that gives life to all creation. Wisdom's relationship to human beings, moreover, is described as one of "delight." This relationship of delight is developed in the final portrait of Wisdom as the ideal wife and mother who cares so well for her household that her husband and children "rise up and call her blessed" (Prov 31:28).

The language of blessedness—the language of beatitude—belongs particularly to the Wisdom writings. The English translation "happy" cannot begin to do justice to the full meaning because happy in modern parlance can apply to a wide range of shallow things. To be "blessed" is unequivocally to share in the divine life.

In the Book of Job

Job is considered a Wisdom book. Yet readers over the centuries have puzzled, "What wisdom does Job find?" On one level, his story seems simplistic: God boasts of Job's piety, and "the Satan," or Adversary, boasts he can destroy that piety by destroying Job's happiness. God agrees to the wager and the Adversary brings one disaster after another upon Job, first wiping out his oxen, sheep, and camels; next his children (1:13-19); and then inflaming his skin from head to toe (2:7). Job survives all these torments without cursing God, and, in the end, God rewards him with another set of oxen, sheep, camels, and children. These events compose the outer, prose frame of the narrative, often referred to as the "folktale" frame. But simply to sum up the story is to miss the point. The heart of the piece lies in the poetry between the prose passages, where Job's friends point out to him how God must be punishing him for some evil he has done, while Job, even at his most despairing, refuses to accept that view of God, of himself, and of suffering. A close look at the text reveals a provocative exploration of different perspectives on these three realities.

Job's friends—Eliphaz, Bildad, and Zophar—offer in different but repetitive ways the conventional view that God rewards virtue and punishes evil. As a consequence, they assume that anyone who suffers like Job, must have brought it upon himself. In chapter 33, another figure named Elihu appears and repeats their arguments. In this perspective, God wields strict justice, the sufferer is guilty, and suffering should be borne as purgative. Job refuses to accept any part of this: he insists he is not guilty, his suffering is unfair, and God would not sanction such injustice. At the same time, Job cries out to God to speak to him and let him know why this is happening to him.

At first reading, the work seems to present an interminable cycle of pain and admonishment, with the admonishment adding to the pain. Yet a second or third reading reveals details that show dramatic shifts in perspective. One of these can be understood as a shift from an Elohist view of God to a Yahwist view—the two different understandings of God that emerge from Genesis 1 through Genesis 3. In the Elohist view, God is remote from human beings, speaking to them through intermediaries; in the Yahwist view, God is close to human beings, communicating with them directly. In the book of Job, those who assume Job's sufferings to be a matter of God's justice have an Elohist perspective. Most of all, Elihu, who sums up the earlier arguments, articulates the idea of God's remoteness. He speaks of how God communicates through dreams (33:15) and messengers (33:23); he notes that neither human righteousness nor human wickedness can affect God (35:6-8, 13-15); he argues, "God is exalted in his power" and greater than we can know (36:22-26). Job, on the other hand, demands that God answer him; above all, he wants to "see" God—that is, experience God directly. His demand reflects the Yahwist view that God is close to us and should answer us as one human person does another. And, in the thirty-eighth chapter, God grants his request. As a whole drama, in other words, the book of Job moves from the Elohist view of Job's friends and Elihu to the Yahwist perspective of Job.

Seen this way, the whole work is about different theologies and their accordingly different views of theodicy. The NRSV speaks of the book of Job as a "symposium," and Donald Kraus calls it a "diatribe"—a genre, he notes, that "in the ancient Near East, as well as in the classical world of Greece and Rome . . . meant a discourse or an argument among various participants."[4] The prose "folktale" opening imagines a shallow God who can boast of Job as a possession and wager away his happiness. Job's friends argue from the perspective of a distant God who deals out punishment for sin, and Elihu speaks explicitly of the unreachableness of God. Job, meanwhile, in all his laments, never accepts this idea of a remote, uncaring, unjust God. He holds steadfastly to the ideas that God is close and benevolent, he himself is innocent, and his suffering cannot be a matter of God's justice. In the end, God engages in dialogue with Job and reproves the others for speaking falsely about God.

One element of the wisdom Job learns, then, is that his idea of God is right. At the same time, he learns all that he does not know about God:

> I have uttered what I did not understand,
>> things too wonderful for me, which I did not know. . . .
> I had heard of you by the hearing of the ear,
>> but now my eye sees you. (42:3, 5)

His direct experience of God leaves him awed and silent. That experience, however, is not one in which he grasps God totally. God, after all, even in speaking to Job, does not answer Job's question about why this suffering has befallen him but responds instead by asking Job how much he knows about Creation. Nonetheless, a great deal is revealed about God in the process.

First, it is noteworthy that God responds to Job at all. Elihu (whose name ironically means "He is my God") has just told Job that human beings are too ignorant to speak to God: "We cannot argue [with God] because we are in darkness. Is anything conveyed

---

4. Donald Kraus, *The Book of Job, Annotated and Explained* (Woodstock, VT: Skylight Paths, 2012), xiii.

to Him when I speak?" (37:19-20; JSB). God's response to Job is in itself the first rebuke to Elihu.

Second, Elihu has argued that it is God's power in thunder and lightning that shows God's inaccessibility to human beings: "God thunders wondrously with his voice; he does great things that we cannot comprehend" (37:5-6). Elihu contemplates the storms of the cosmos in order to prove to Job that God is unattainable: "The Almighty—we cannot find him" (37:23). To Elihu, God is outside the universe, causing storms to happen, "Whether for correction, or for his land, or for love" (37:13). It is therefore significant that God speaks to Job "*out of* the storm"—that is, not as one manipulating the world from outside but as one living within it. God is at the heart of the storm, sharing it with God's creatures.

Next, when God describes the cosmos, the description reveals many sides to God beyond thundering power. "Where were you," God asks Job, "when the morning stars sang together, and all the heavenly beings shouted for joy?" (38:4-7). By implication, beauty and joy come from God. Also, tender caring for every creature: "Who provides for the raven its prey, when its young ones cry to God and wander about for lack of food?" (38:41). Most significantly, God is the source of human wisdom: "Who has put wisdom in the inward parts, or given understanding to the mind?" (38:36). By implication, God is not the remote manipulator of human beings but one who shares with them the divine wisdom.

This last aspect of God is in fact dramatized in God's very speech to Job. God has taken Job seriously enough to answer him. In that answer, God sets forth the marvels of the universe; Job's experience is not unlike that of those privileged figures in later literature who ascend though the heavens to be shown the secrets of the cosmos. Job, of course, does not ascend but descends into misery. Nonetheless, he too is the recipient of revelations—not the least of which is God's willingness to share with him.

Is Job transformed in any way by this experience? In terms of the whole work, both Job and God are transformed in the ending.

It may be strange to think of God being transformed, but certainly the portrayal of God in the end is different from the portrayal of God in the beginning. In the final speeches, God is no longer a shallow figure who boasts about a creature and places a wager on him. Instead, God reproaches those who have spoken falsely about God as one who punishes with suffering, and God praises the truthfulness of "my servant Job" (42:7). In recognition of Job's true piety—as distinct from the mouthed pieties of the others—God asks Job to pray for his unenlightened friends (42:8).

What of Job? The author suggests subtle stages in Job's transformation. At first, Job is simply silenced: "See, I am of small account, what shall I answer you? I lay my hand on my mouth" (40:4). Next, he recognizes all he does not know: "I have uttered what I did not understand, things too wonderful for me, which I did not know" (42:3). In both of these speeches, the author dramatizes the recurring theme of the Wisdom books: "Fear of the Lord is the beginning of Wisdom." Here, of course, "fear" does not mean fright but awe. Awe before the mystery of God is what opens the human being to new understanding: "Hear, and I will speak; I will question you, and you declare to me" (42:4). Job desired to "see" God, and now he has: "I had heard of you with the hearing of the ear, but now my eye sees you" (42:5). That mystical insight dissolves Job's ego: "[T]herefore I despise myself, and repent in dust and ashes" (42:6).

It is easy to read the prose ending as merely showing Job's lot expanded in quantifiable terms: Job's brothers and sisters and friends all bring him gifts, and "the Lord blessed the latter days of Job more than his beginning" (42:11-12). But far more important is Job's way of relating to his children, especially his daughters. He no longer makes sacrifices for them just in case they have sinned, as he did before (1:5). And he gives his daughters wildly frivolous, playful names: "Dove," "Cinnamon," and "Horn of Eye-Shadow." Clearly, Job has lightened up! He no longer exhibits the heavy piety of one who thinks he can control God through his sacrifices. Instead, he imitates God's loving, sometimes whimsical, creativity. Job's circumstances are the same as at the beginning; the change in Job is *within*.

The final mark of his transformation is his giving estates to these daughters along with their brothers (42:14)—an unheard of procedure in ancient times. The significance may be tied to the fact that Wisdom in these traditions is always personified as a woman. Perhaps the author intended the elevation of women in society, and of the feminine in general, should be seen as an intrinsic part of what it means to be wise.

In spite of the separation of centuries and cultures, there is an essential link between the insights of the book of Job and the writings of Teilhard. Both find the divine presence in creation, in the matter of the earth. The author of Job, like Teilhard, sees God not as an outsider to the Earth but as one within it. Each writer rejects the idea of a good God commanding or even allowing evil and poses instead the idea of a creating God who suffers in and through the process of creation. What Job learns is the wisdom of the Earth, and that is the divine presence in all things. For Job, as for Teilhard, that divine presence is personal and close, constantly communicating wisdom to human beings. Human beings are naturally disposed to respond, to share in the divine life. In the ancient wisdom of Job, as in the modern thought of Teilhard, the human idea of God and the wisdom of the human being simultaneously evolve.

Further Reflections

Does this study of Wisdom have practical implications for Christians living today? I think it does. I think it compels us to reconsider our present spiritual state in relation to both our past and our future. In respect to our past, it should move us to cherish our roots in Judaism and value its many paths to Wisdom. Reading the Jewish Wisdom texts in the light of Teilhard's evolutionary vision, we can see how much we owe to them our awe of creation and our perception of a divine presence at the core of our being. Understanding them in Teilhard's framework should also bring us to acknowledge that their expressions of Wisdom, along with our own, are still evolving.

We can see how much we share the elements of that evolutionary framework, that insistent thrust towards the future: the longing to see God's face, to ascend to an ultra-human sphere, to be transformed by God's word.

We need to grasp that thrust towards a transformed future in Paul's emphasis on human dynamism, in the Creed's proclamation of trust in a future not yet achieved, in the gospels' invitation to transform ourselves into a word of mutual empathy, forgiveness, and service. In short, we need to develop a spirituality that begins by acknowledging our incompleteness, and a praxis of empathy that is rooted in our longing to work towards the evolution of the wholeness of humanity.

Works Cited

Armstrong, Karen. *The Case For God*. New York: Grove Press, 2007.

————. *The Great Transformation*. New York: Alfred A. Knopf, 2006.

Athanasius. *Against the Arians*, 82.2.

Augustine. *Sermon 2, on Matthew 3:13*.

Berlin, Adele, and Marc Zvi Brettler, eds. *The Jewish Study Bible*. New York: Oxford University Press, 2004.

Boyarin, Daniel. *Intertextuality and the Reading of Midrash*. Bloomington, IN: University of Indiana Press, 1990.

Brettler, Marc Zvi, and Adele Berlin, eds. *The Jewish Study Bible*. New York: Oxford University Press, 2004.

Brettler, Marc Zvi, and Amy-Jill Levine, eds. *The Jewish Annotated New Testament*. New York: Oxford University Press, 2011.

Brocke, Michael, and Jakob J. Petuchowski, eds. *The Lord's Prayer and Jewish Liturgy*. New York: Seabury Press, 1978.

Brown, Raymond. *The Virginal Conception and Bodily Resurrection of Christ*. New York: Paulist Press, 1973.

————. *The Gospel of John*. New York: Doubleday, 1970.

Brownson, James, James H. Charlesworth, M. T. Davis, Steven J. Kraftchick, and Alan Segal, eds. *The Messiah: Developments in Earliest Judaism and Christianity*. The First Princeton Symposium on Judaism and Christian Origins. Minneapolis: Fortress Press, 1992.

Brueggemann, Walter. *Praying the Psalms*. Eugene, OR: Cascade Books, 2007.

————. *Divine Presence Amid Violence*. Eugene, OR: Cascade Books, 2009.

Charlesworth, James H., M. T. Davis, Steven J. Kraftchick, and Alan Segal, eds. *The Messiah: Developments in Earliest Judaism and Christianity.* The First Princeton Symposium on Judaism and Christian Origins. Minneapolis: Fortress Press, 1992.

Charlesworth, James H., ed. *The Old Testament Pseudepigrapha*, vol. 1. Garden City, NY: Doubleday, 1983.

Chilton, Bruce, and Jacob Neusner. *Judaism in the New Testament.* New York: Routledge, 1995.

Crossan, J. D. *The Power of Parable.* San Francisco: Harper One, 2012.

Davis, Ellen. "Job and Jacob: The Integrity of Faith." In *Reading Between the Texts: Intertextuality and the Hebrew Bible*, edited by Donna Nolan Fewell. Louisville, KY: Westminster Press, 1992.

Davis, M. T., James Brownson, James H. Charlesworth, Steven J. Kraftchick, and Alan Segal, eds. *The Messiah: Developments in Earliest Judaism and Christianity.* The First Princeton Symposium on Judaism and Christian Origins. Minneapolis: Fortress Press, 1992.

Donahue, John. *The Gospel in Parable.* Philadelphia: Fortress Press, 1988.

Fewell, Donna Nolan, ed. *Reading Between the Texts: Intertextuality and the Hebrew Bible.* Louisville, KY: Westminster Press, 1992.

Fishbane, Michael. *Biblical Interpretation in Ancient Israel.* New York: Oxford University Press, 1985.

———. *The Garments of Torah: Essays in Biblical Hermeneutics.* Bloomington, IN: University of Indiana Press, 1989.

———. "Inner-Biblical Exegesis." In *Midrash and Literature*, edited by Geoffrey Hartman and Sanford Budick. New Haven: Yale University Press, 1986.

Frerichs, Ernest S., William Scott Green, and Jacob Neusner, eds. *Judaisms and Their Messiahs at the Turn of the Christian Era.* Cambridge, England: Cambridge University Press, 1987.

Genesis Rabbah, Introduction.

Glenn, Linda MacDonald. In *National Geographic*, April 2017.

Green, Arthur, and Barry W. Holtz, eds. *Your Word Is Fire.* New York: Paulist Press, 1977.

Green, William Scott, Ernest S. Frerichs, and Jacob Neusner, eds. *Judaisms and Their Messiahs at the Turn of the Christian Era.* Cambridge, England: Cambridge University Press, 1987.

Himmelfarb, Martha. *Ascent to Heaven in Jewish and Christian Apocalypses.* New York: Oxford University Press, 1993.

Holtz, Barry W., and Arthur Green, eds. *Judaisms and Their Messiahs at the Turn of the Christian Era.* Cambridge, England: Cambridge University Press, 1987.

Isaac, E. In James Charlesworth, ed., *The Old Testament Pseudepigrapha,* vol. 1. Garden City, NY: Doubleday, 1983.

Jeremias, Joachim. *The Central Meaning of the New Testament.* New York: Charles Scribner, 1965.

Jewish Annotated New Testament. Marc Zvi Brettler and Amy-Jill Levine, eds. New York: Oxford University Press, 2011.

Jewish Study Bible. Adele Berlin and Marc Zvi Brettler, eds. New York: Oxford University Press, 2004.

Kraftchick, Steven J., James Brownson, James H. Charlesworth, M. T. Davis, and Alan Segal, eds. *The Messiah: Developments in Earliest Judaism and Christianity.* The First Princeton Symposium on Judaism and Christian Origins. Minneapolis: Fortress Press, 1992.

Kraus, Donald. *The Book of Job, Annotated and Explained.* Woodstock, VT: Skylight Paths, 2012.

Kugel, James. *The Bible as It Was.* Cambridge, MA: Harvard University Press, 1997.

Kurzwell, Ray. *The Singularity Is Near.* New York: Viking Press, 2005.

Levenson, Jon. *The Death and Resurrection of the Beloved Son.* New Haven: Yale University Press, 1993.

Levine, Amy-Jill, and Marc Zvi Brettler, eds. *The Jewish Annotated New Testament.* New York: Oxford University Press, 2004.

Max, D. T., "Beyond Human." In *National Geographic,* April 2017.

Moore, Stephen. *Mark and Method. New Approaches in Biblical Studies.* Minneapolis: Fortress Press, 1992.

Neusner, Jacob, and Bruce Chilton. *Judaism in the New Testament.* New York: Routledge, 1995.

Neusner, Jacob, William Scott Green, and Ernest S. Frerichs, eds. *Judaisms and Their Messiahs at the Turn of the Christian Era.* Cambridge, England: Cambridge University Press, 1987.

Pramuk, Christopher. *At Play in Creation: Merton's Awakening to the Feminine Divine.* Collegeville, MN: Liturgical Press, 2015.

————. *Sophia: The Hidden Christ of Thomas Merton.* Collegeville, MN: Liturgical Press, 2009.

Segal, Alan, James Brownson, James H. Charlesworth, M. T. Davis, and Steven J. Kraftchick, eds. *The Messiah: Developments in Earliest Judaism and Christianity.* The First Princeton Symposium on Judaism and Christian Origins. Minneapolis: Fortress Press, 1992.

Sholem, Gershom. *Major Trends in Jewish Mysticism.* New York: Schocken Books, 1941; reprint, 1993.

Sifre on Lev 26:12.

Smith, Mark. *God in Translation. Deities in Cross-Cultural Discourse in the Biblical World.* Tubingen: Mohr and Siebeck, 2008.

Song of Songs Rabbah, Introduction.

Taylor, Vincent. *The Gospel According to Saint Mark.* London: Macmillan, 1963.

Teilhard de Chardin, Pierre. *Christianity and Evolution.* Translated by René Hague. New York: Harcourt Brace Jovanovich, 1971.

————. *The Divine Milieu: An Essay on the Interior Life.* Translated by William Collins. New York : Harper Perennial, 2001.

————. *The Future of Man.* Translated by Norman Denny. New York: Doubleday, 2004.

————. *The Heart of Matter.* Translated by René Hague. New York: Harcourt Brace Jovanovich, 1978.

————. *The Phenomenon of Man.* Translated by Bernard Wall. New York: Harper and Brothers, 1959.

————. *Writings in Time of War.* Translated by René Hague. New York: Harper and Row, 1968.

Wellhausen, Julius. *Prolegomena to the History of Ancient Israel.* 1882.

Wiesel, Elie. *Night.* New York: Hill and Wang, 2006.

Wrede, William. *The Messianic Secret.* Translated by J. C. Grieg. Greenwood, SC: Attic Press, 1971.

Index of Authors and Subjects

Index of Sacred Texts